WASHINGTON'S
RAIL-TRAILS

D1016093

WASHINGTON'S

RAIL-TRAILS

A Guide for Walkers, Bicyclists, Equestrians

Fred Wert

THE
MOUNTAINEERS

© Text, maps, photos 1992 by Fred Wert

4
5 4

Published by **The Mountaineers**
1011 SW Klickitat Way, Seattle, Washington 98134

Published simultaneously in Canada by **Douglas & McIntyre, Ltd.**, 1615 Venables Street, Vancouver, B.C. V5L 2H1

Published simultaneously in Great Britain by **Cordee**, 3a DeMontfort Street, Leicester, England, LE1 7HD

Manufactured in the United States of America

Cover photograph by Fred Wert
All other photographs by Fred Wert
Maps by Fred Wert
Edited by Linda Gunnarson
Cover design by Betty Watson
Book design by Bridget Culligan Design

Frontispiece: *Equestrians emerge from the east portal of the Boylston Tunnel.*

Library of Congress Cataloging-in-Publication Data

Wert, Fred, 1949–
  Washington's rail-trails / Fred Wert.
    p.   cm.
  Includes index.
  ISBN 0-89886-299-X
  1. Trails—Washington (State)—Guide-books.   2. Outdoor
recreation—Washington (State)—Guide-books.   3. Washington (State)-
-Description and travel—1981- —Guide-books.   I. Title.
  GV191.42.W2W47   1992   91-33507
  796.5′09797—dc20   CIP

PREFACE

An important part of Washington's history is quietly disappearing. As the result of economic pressure, many railroad lines are being abandoned throughout the state. Railroads were the first major transportation system developed in Washington, and they were critical for its economic development. Ironically, it is now economics that is slowly eroding their importance as a transportation system.

Thousands of miles of railroads were built throughout Washington, from main-line routes still operating to short logging lines that existed just long enough to get the trees out. The construction of these railroads significantly altered the shape of the land by making narrow, flat strips of railway bed. When the railroad companies leave, they take with them the rails, ties, and trains. But the railroad beds, the graded dirt and gravel, the long narrow strips of smooth land, remain. Looking closely, one can see these abandoned rights-of-way everywhere: along rivers and streams, in second-growth forests, behind urban warehouses, in the routing of country roads, and concealed under freeways. Some people view these corridors as scars upon the land. But more and more people are seeing them as an opportunity to create rail-trails— public-access trails built on abandoned railroad rights-of-way.

Rail-trails serve many public needs. They certainly provide recreational opportunities for a wide range of nonmotorized uses, more than any other kind of trail. They preserve unique greenspace, contributing to the green aesthetic that is so much a part of the natural beauty of Washington. They also keep alive the last vestiges of railroad history in a more visible and active way than the few remaining steam engines displayed at local parks. Rail-trails provide a public connection between public parks and open space in a way roads can never achieve. And they may well serve future needs as public corridors for high-speed rail or, if oil reserves are depleted, low-speed nonmotorized use.

There is a sense of urgency in developing rail-trails. Once a railroad abandons operations the land can revert to many owners, and it may be very difficult to reassemble the same corridor of land from numerous small parcels. The result can be very daunting to government agencies, even if they do have an interest in the rail-trail concept.

It is the goal of this book to increase public awareness of existing rail-trails, their singular and wonderful qualities, and the opportunities for further rail-trail development in Washington State. Timing is critical, and it is hoped that this book will help citizens realize what a valuable resource rail-trails are and help to ensure the continued development of all potential rail-trails. Now is the time for citizens and public officials to take action, or this resource will be lost forever.

Fred Wert, *Seattle, 1992*

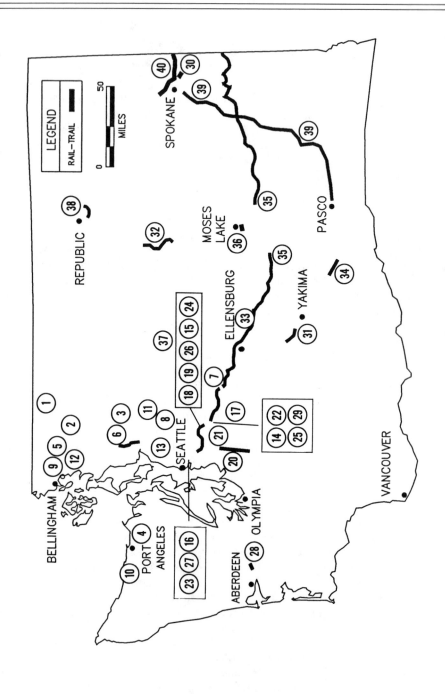

CONTENTS

INTRODUCTION

Throughout Washington abandoned railroad rights-of-way are being converted to nonmotorized trails for public recreation. These "rail-trails" are a valuable addition to the public trails of this state. They are linear parks, publicly accessible corridors that preserve open space, provide wildlife habitat, and serve as a valuable recreational resource. When most peple think of trails they think of mountain trails that are steep, narrow, and rugged. Rail-trails are different. They are wide, have very gentle grades, and occur generally in lowland areas near cities and water.

A rail-trail is a public access trail constructed on an abandoned railroad right-of-way or adjacent to an existing railroad. Its condition can vary from a rugged, overgrown dirt path to 12-foot-wide pavement with restrooms, benches, trailheads, and viewpoints. Conversion of these abandoned railroad rights-of-way into rail-trails provides wonderful and unique opportunities for walking, running, bicycling, horseback riding, and many other human-powered activities. Their special features make them ideal as multiple-use trails.

Washington State has been a pioneer in the development of rail-trails. The Burke-Gilman Trail and the King County Interurban Trail

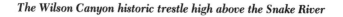

The Wilson Canyon historic trestle high above the Snake River

both opened in the early 1970s, and now there are more than forty rail-trails in the state. Washington also has the nation's longest rail-trail. The combination of Iron Horse State Park and the Milwaukee Road Corridor Trail stretches more than 300 miles across the state from Cedar Falls near North Bend to the Idaho border.

Rail-trails are being developed throughout the nation at an accelerating pace as railway companies continue abandoning rights-of-way and citizen action groups seize the opportunity to create rail-trails. There are about 500 rail-trails nationally, covering more than 5,000 miles, with many more rail-trails planned for development in the next few years.

Rail-trails vary in their location from urban cities to lowland forests, from wide, paved surfaces to rough rock ballast, from urban connectors to scenic vistas. Part of their attraction is that they traverse lowland areas normally closed in winter to nonmotorized users. They are also efficient bicycle routes, safe places to gallop horses and pull wagons, and safe winter recreation areas.

Unique Features of Rail-Trails

Rail-trails are not like most other trails. They have many characteristics that make them unique:

- **The route already exists.** A converted railroad grade provides an established, feasible route. This saves considerable time and money for the trail's managing agency. One of the primary reasons that most of the rail-trails in this book exist is because the abandoned railroad grade provided a ready-made and obvious trail.
- **The trail is already built.** Since the rails and ties usually have been removed by the departing railway company, the remaining rail bed is immediately usable as a trail. Sometimes the surface is modified by the addition of smaller gravel or paving, but essentially the trail is ready for use. This is distinctly different from trying to carve a trail through the woods or between urban developments.
- **Rail-trails have gentle grades.** Railroads were built at minimum inclines, with most main-line grades never exceeding a 2.2 percent grade and logging railroads seldom exceeding 4 percent. Compared to many backcountry trails, rail-trails are flat and smooth with very gentle grades.
- **They provide excellent nonmotorized transportation routes.** Communities were built around railroad lines, and when railroad rights-of-way are turned into rail-trails, they connect the communities. In King County, the Burke-Gilman Trail and the

King County Interurban Trail are both excellent examples of routes used by people commuting by bicycle or foot to work.

- **They can provide revenue for operating agencies.** Several agencies have contracts with AT&T that permit AT&T to put their fiber-optics lines underground next to rail-trails. This provides income for parks departments that can be used in the maintenance and operation of rail-trails.
- **They provide recreational opportunities for special-needs trail users.** The elderly and physically impaired, small children riding bicycles, babies in baby carriages, and horse-drawn wagons all need a wide path with a gentle grade. Rail-trails are unique in that some of them can provide a safe, easy route for a variety of special-needs trail users.
- **They can provide access roads for utility corridors.** Many railroad routes are used by electric utilities for voltage transmission lines. Rail-trails can offer improved access to these lines using standard trucks.
- **They can serve as dikes along rivers and oceans.** Because railroads required gentle grades, many were built near rivers and streams, following the gentle inclines of natural waterways.
- **They preserve historic structures.** As part of the development of rail-trails many old railway structures are being preserved, especially old railway stations. There are also several significant railroad trestles and other structures in Washington that are protected by the State Historic Preservation Act.
- **They provide economic opportunities for some towns.** People who use rail-trails do so primarily for recreation and are willing to travel to good recreation spots. In Wisconsin, for example, the Elroy–Sparta Trail has greatly helped three small railway towns that were dying when the tracks were removed. Now the towns are being revitalized by serving the rail-trail users who travel from Chicago and other places to use the rail-trail. Similar opportunities exist in Washington State.
- **They preserve wildlife habitat.** The 50-to-200-foot-wide corridors created by railroads often have not been disturbed for several decades and in some places are the only undeveloped land. The preservation of this land provides wildlife habitat that might not otherwise exist. A good example of this is the King County Interurban Trail, which is surrounded by warehouses but also includes considerable wetlands supporting many mammals, reptiles, birds, and insects.
- **They provide numerous access points.** Many long-distance, back-country mountain trails have few access points. Rail-trails are primarily located in lowland areas, and population centers were

Washington State Railroads

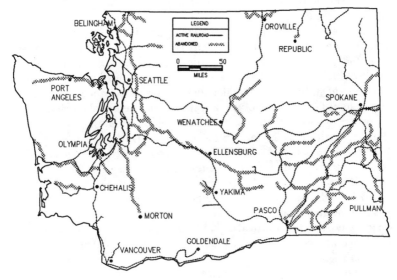

built up around them. Often they have many access points where public roads cross them, and thus it is easy to use just part of the entire trail length.

The many unique features of rail-trails are only now being realized by trail managers and trail users. The development of a system of rail-trails throughout Washington may well make them the state's most popular trails in the future.

Railroad History

Railroads were the first major transportation systems across the nation and around the state. They served as the first reliable high-speed transportation service for both freight and people and were an important reason for Washington's rapid growth at the turn of the century. Many railroads were built specifically for logging or mining, the remnants of which can still be seen by the careful observer.

At one time there were more than 5,000 miles of interstate railroad lines in Washington, with several more thousand miles of logging and mining railroads. With the increased use of trucks, some railroad lines have gradually become uneconomical. It is less expensive and more flexible to haul for short distances and move lightweight goods by truck. Consequently, since 1970 more than 1,800 miles of railroads have been abandoned, with many more miles scheduled to be abandoned in the next few years. The accompanying map shows the locations of the active and abandoned main-line railroads throughout the state as of 1991.

Railroads left their mark on the landscape as many cities and towns were built alongside the tracks. Many communities were deserted long ago, and all signs of civilization disappeared except for the railway grades. Some of the place names mentioned in this book are those of old railroad stations and may not show up on modern maps, especially state highway maps. Several rail-trails are named for the original railroads. The Spruce Railroad Trail was named after the railway built during World War II to harvest valuable stands of spruce on the Olympic Peninsula. The Milwaukee Road Corridor Trail was named after the common name for the Chicago, Milwaukee, St. Paul, and Pacific Railroad.

This book does not try to document every trail that exists on a railroad right-of-way in Washington. There are thousands of miles of abandoned logging railroads; many of these are now motor-vehicle roads, and some are parts of hiking trails. This book concentrates on rail-trails specifically built on main-line or interstate commerce railroad rights-of-way and on those where there has been significant trail development.

How Rail-Trails Are Created

Citizen action groups create rail-trails when they see the opportunity to turn an abandoned railway grade into a nonmotorized path. The public is often first aware that a railroad is being abandoned when the rails and ties are removed. This is also the time when most people consider using the abandoned right-of-way for trail purposes. To embark on the conversion procedure it is critical to have a thorough understanding of the abandonment process.

Why railroads are abandoned

Main-line railroads that conduct interstate commerce are all regulated by the Interstate Commerce Commission (ICC). The ICC controls not only the operation of active lines but also their abandonment. Since the railroads that serve shippers have a monopoly on the rail business along a specific line, the ICC makes sure that railroads do not charge excessive rates or close down a line without notice. The theory is that they serve a public good in providing rail service.

The economics of transportation have changed greatly from the days when railroads were being built. At the turn of the century there were very few roads and no trucks. Now there is considerable competition from both truck and water transport. The result is less railroad

An old railroad passenger car near Kahlotus

traffic, and some lines are becoming less profitable. When a railroad decides that it is losing money on a particular section of track, it can file a formal legal request to the ICC to request permission to stop providing service and to abandon that section of track. The ICC normally approves such requests without a hearing unless there are comments or complaints filed by shippers on the line to be abandoned or from other interested parties.

Rail-banking

The 1983 National Trails Act added another option to abandonment of a railroad line. This act makes it possible for the ICC to "rail-bank" a railroad line instead of declaring it abandoned. When the ICC declares a line abandoned, this means that the railroad can stop serving shippers, discontinue tariffs, and pull up the rails and ties. It also means that any easements the railroad has to use other parties' lands for railroad purposes terminate. A "railroad easement" is a legal interest (like a lease) for use of a piece of land contingent upon the land being used for railroad purposes. If a railroad ceases operations, its interest in the land returns to the holder of the easement, usually the heirs of the original easement with the railroad but sometimes also the current adjacent landowner.

Rail-banking does not involve legal abandonment of the line. The ICC allows the railroad to discontinue tariffs, remove rails and ties, and sell the land that the railroad owns. The purchaser of the land under rail-banking has to agree that in the future, should a railroad company want to use the line for railroad purposes, the purchaser will sell back the land for railroad purposes. The interim property owner also must agree that the right-of-way will be used for trail purposes.

Rail-banking is a powerful tool for government agencies planning to acquire a railroad right-of-way for a trail. This is because the agency can acquire all the land the railroad is using without any land reverting to adjacent property owners who have an underlying interest. The alternative—necessary if the railroad abandons the line—is to purchase individual parcels of land from many individual landowners, a very difficult and expensive undertaking.

Developing rail-trails

The development of rail-trails is different from the development of other public park or recreation-facility projects. Most often only a few people know in advance that a railroad is going to remove the rails and ties and abandon a line. Once this has happened, it may be too late to begin converting this once no-man's-land railroad right-of-way to a pathway through the city or the country.

The first, and often the most difficult, step is the acquisition of the railroad right-of-way. As mentioned above, it is critical for the potential rail-trail developer to be ready before the railroad applies to the ICC for abandonment so that the agency can request rail-banking. Part of this preparation is to have public support for the project and the trail route in the agency's planning documents. The agency should also request to be notified by the railroad of any pending abandonments.

Agency plans

Most rail-trails are built by public agencies. These agencies provide public facilities for citizens and are usually stable, continuing entities. Usually, it is the local parks departments that get involved in developing rail-trails, although public-works departments may also play a part. An important aspect of any agency's work is to prepare planning documents, especially for new or expanded capital projects. These documents require the approval of elected officials and are the road map and authority for agency staff to proceed. They are also important for gaining public input and for applying for funding to the state's Interagency Committee for Outdoor Recreation.

Trail funding

Funding is a major challenge in developing rail-trails. The first requirement is acquisition funds. The cost of acquiring a railroad right-of-way varies considerably, depending on whether the railroad property is located in a downtown urban area or on marginal land, for example. The cost for many projects amounts to several hundred thousand dollars, which is higher than the cost of many park-acquisition projects.

Another funding problem arises from the fact that rail-trails are a new type of park project. Many park department directors get a tremendous amount of pressure from the public—from very well organized and vocal groups—for more baseball, soccer, golf, and tennis facilities. Also, there is no history of rail-trail development for many city, county, or state agencies to consult for guidance.

However, there are funding opportunities for rail-trails other than the traditional sources available for parks and recreation facilities. Because they are linear and continuous, rail-trails make excellent sites for a variety of utilities. Often the utilities find the acquisition of a continuous corridor of land far less expensive than trying to create a new corridor. The installation of power lines, fiber-optics cables, water lines, and sewers is perfectly compatible with rail-trail development. In some cases utility companies buy the land and prepare the trail surfaces as part of their use of the land.

A new source of funding has been created by the Washington Wildlife and Recreation Coalition. This nonprofit statewide organization was formed solely to get legislative approval of millions of dollars for the acquisition and development of wildlife and recreation land throughout the state. A small portion of this funding is reserved for trails. As important a recreational resource as trails are to the people of Washington, this is the first time there has been a dedicated funding source for trails, and it provides a viable source for rail-trail funding.

Trail design

Once a right-of-way has been acquired, the next step is to design the rail-trail and decide what type of improvements will be made. This process sometimes includes a master plan of the entire project that identifies the route, trailhead sites, and the trail surface design. An important part of the design phase is the development of a trail management plan. This plan considers all of the concerns of the trail manager, adjacent property owners, trail users, and emergency services personnel.

Trail construction

The last major phase of rail-trail development is construction. This is usually a straightforward process. Often it is easier to get acquisition funds than construction funds. One alternative for the trail manager is to involve user groups that are willing to volunteer to help in construction, thus reducing costs and opening a rail-trail to the public more quickly. Several user groups have been active in trail construction in Washington State, including the Backcountry Horsemen of Washington, The Mountaineers, Volunteers for Outdoor Washington, and the Backcountry Bicycle Trails Club.

The History and Future of Rail-Trails

The first rail-trails were developed in the late 1960s and early 1970s. The creation of these pioneering rail-trails was difficult because there were many questions regarding who would use them and what kinds of problems would develop. Yet most rail-trails have become dramatic successes, with high-volume usage and few management problems. The value of rail-trails has become more apparent in recent years. In 1987, the President's Commission on the American Outdoors recommended that "thousands of miles of abandoned railroads be converted to public use." Many articles have appeared about rail-trails in national magazines and local newspapers, and state and local agencies are learning that they serve as ideal public recreation facilities.

Washington State has been a significant participant in this movement. The Burke-Gilman Trail in Seattle opened in 1976, making it one of the first rail-trails in the United States. Today it serves more than one million users per year. The state has more than forty rail-trails open to the public, covering more than 550 miles. They vary in length from half-mile-long sidewalks to a 300-mile route across the eastern part of the state.

There is a tremendous amount of support for rail-trails in Washington. The parks departments in Seattle, King County, and Bellingham

New paving near Snohomish

have been building rail-trails for years. Surveys by counties also show that the most popular outdoor recreational activities are predominantly trail-use activities. The State Comprehensive Outdoor Recreation Planning (SCORP) Program includes a 1987 survey of outdoor recreation in Washington. Among the top-ranked recreational activities were jogging/running (first), walking in neighborhood parks (second), bicycling on the road (sixth), day hiking (twelfth), nature study and wildlife observation (sixteenth), and bicycling off the road (twenty-ninth). A good indication of the public's support for continued development is passage of the 1989 King County open-space bond issue. This public bond issue passed by 82 percent and allocated $31 million for rail-trails and lowland trail development.

At the state level, several agencies manage rail-trails. The Washington State Parks and Recreation Commission is presently pursuing acquisition of more railroad rights-of-way for long-distance trails. The 1991 State Trails Plan also supports the creation of rail-trails. It calls for State Parks to take the lead in creating rail-trails, adding another 450 miles of rail-trails and completing the Washington Cross-State Trail by the year 2000.

Future rail-trails

There are a number of rail-trails planned for future development. An important project that has tremendous public support is the Pierce County Foothills Trail. This trail will start near Orting and go to Buckley, Wilkerson, and Carbanado in the foothills to the north of Mount Rainier. It is part of a system of Pierce County trails that will connect the populated urban areas with Mount Rainier.

Another major rail-trail project is the Olympic Discovery Trail. This rail-trail will cover 50 miles between Port Townsend and Port Angeles on the Olympic Peninsula. It is still in the early planning stages but has considerable public support and interest.

Other rail-trail projects are in various stages of acquisition, planning, or development. These include:

Bay to Baker Rail-Trail	Lacey–Offut Lake Trail
Black Diamond Trail	Lake Union Bikeway
Cedar River Trail	North King County Interurban Trail
Chehalis–South Bay Trail	Palouse Pathway
Chelatchie Prairie Trail	Sedro Wooley–Arlington Trail
Clayton Beach Trail	Similkameen Trail
Darrington Trail	Skagit River Trail
East Lake Sammamish Trail	Spokane–Newport Trail
Enumclaw Trail	White River–Palmer Trail
Everett–Shoreline Interurban Trail	Woodard Bay Trail
Iron Goat Trail	Yelm–Tenino Trail
Klickitat Trail	

Proposed rail-trails

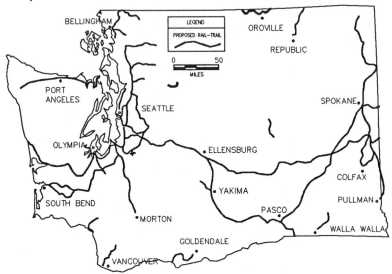

More information on these planned rail-trails is included in Appendix 2, Future Rail-Trails.

New rail-trails are being considered and constructed at an increasing pace as the demand for lowland trails increases. An attempt was made here to mention most of the rail-trail projects that are going on in Washington at this time. If you know of other existing or planned rail-trails, please let the author know by forwarding the information through The Mountaineers Books.

Proposed rail-trails

One purpose of this book is to show the location of rail-trails in Washington State and to entice people to use rail-trails. It is hoped that by using rail-trails the public will understand their exceptional value and work to encourage the development of a complete statewide system of rail-trails for the enjoyment of Washington residents and visitors from other states and countries.

There are already more than 1,800 miles of abandoned railroad rights-of-way in the state, with many more becoming available in the next few years. Together they create an opportunity for developing a complete system of interconnecting rail-trails throughout Washington.

The accompanying map illustrates the author's proposal for a statewide system of rail-trails. This proposal developed around existing rail-trails, abandoned lines, and lines that will likely be abandoned. Many parts of this proposed system are either already open to the pub-

Washington Cross-State Trail

lic or plans are currently under way for developing a rail-trail. Together they can be developed into an interconnecting system of lowland trails throughout the state. An example of how this is working is the Washington Cross-State Trail.

The Washington Cross-State Trail

Imagine walking, riding horseback, or bicycling all the way across Washington State on a nonmotorized path! This dream is becoming a reality with the development of the Washington Cross-State Trail, a series of rail-trails connecting the Pacific Ocean and Idaho. Already about 70 percent of the proposed route is in public ownership. The most extensive portions open for public use are the Milwaukee Road Corridor Trail from Tekoa to the Columbia River and Iron Horse State Park from the Columbia River to Cedar Falls near North Bend. There are plans to add more miles westward in the next few years.

The interest in long-distance trails is becoming greater as more people look for places to enjoy the outdoors. There are now eight long-distance trail routes in the United States that are part of the National Scenic Trail System. Washington State has one National Scenic Trail, the Pacific Crest Scenic Trail, that runs along the crest of the Cascade and Sierra Nevada ranges. There is also a proposal for a Pacific Northwest Trail that would cross the northern part of the state. One drawback is that both routes are under snow most of the year, and many portions of the trails are open only to backpacking and horse travel.

The Washington Cross-State Trail would create a new world of long-distance trail possibilities, one that would be much more accessible to many people and open year-round.

The main route of the Washington Cross-State Trail passes through the towns of Tekoa, Rosalia, Warden, Othello, Ellensburg, South Cle Elum, Cedar Falls, Enumclaw, Buckley, Centralia, Chehalis, and South Bend. There will be a spur into Seattle, and another through Spokane to Idaho. The following table outlines the existing individual trails that make up the Washington Cross-State Trail.

Washington Cross-State Trail		
	SEGMENT	OWNER/MANAGER
Washington Cross-State Trail	Foothills Trail	Pierce County
	Snoqualmie Pass Trail	State Parks
	Iron Horse State Park	State Parks
	Milwaukee Road Corridor Trail	Department of Natural Resources
Seattle Spur Trail	Myrtle Edwards Park Trail	City of Seattle
	Interbay Bike Trail	City of Seattle
	Burke-Gilman Trail	City of Seattle, King County
	Sammamish Slough Trail	King County Parks
	Issaquah Trail	City of Issaquah
	Issaquah Creek Trail	King County Parks
	Preston–Snoqualmie Trail	King County Parks
	Snoqualmie–Cedar Falls Trail	King County Parks
Spokane Spur Trail	Scablands Nature Corridor	State Parks
	Spokane–Fish Lake Trail	City of Spokane
	Spokane River Centennial Trail	State Parks

The completion of the Washington Cross-State Trail will take the cooperation of many agencies. The Washington State Parks and Recreation Commission has taken a leadership role in this project. The State Trails Plan calls for completion of the Washington Cross-State Trail by the year 2000, with State Parks as the lead agency. The accompanying map illustrates the proposed route of the Washington Cross-State Trail.

It is conceivable that the Washington Cross-State Trail could connect through northern Idaho and Montana and help the development of the Trans-Continental Trail (TCT) stretching from the Pacific to the Atlantic Oceans. Citizen groups are already working in Idaho and Montana on sections of this route that could link with the North Country Trail that is currently being developed between North Dakota and New York. The Trans-Continental Trail would be a valuable addition to our nation's National Scenic Trails System.

How You Can Help Build Rail-Trails

There are several ways in which you can help build rail-trails. You can help organize or join a local citizen group that supports a specific rail-trail. Most rail-trail projects are local endeavors developed by cities or counties, and local support is critical to their success. The most successful rail-trails have had strong local coalitions formed solely to encourage their development. These include:

> Lake Union Ship Canal Coalition
> Cowiche Canyon Conservancy
> Lower Yakima Pathway Coalition
> Peninsula Trails Coalition
> Pierce County Foothills Rails-to-Trails Coalition
> Snohomish–Arlington Centennial Trail Coalition
> Spokane River Centennial Trail Committee

You can talk to your elected city, county, and state officials and take them to where the proposed rail-trail will be constructed. Since these projects are usually government-sponsored, it is vital to get the appropriate local agency and elected officials excited about rail-trails. The best way to do this is to take them for a walk on an existing rail-trail and show them the wonderful experience that rail-trails provide.

You can encourage user groups to which you belong to support the development of rail-trails. Many user groups have an interest in trails. The following are some organizations that support rail-trails in Washington State:

> Backcountry Bicycle Trails Club
> Backcountry Horsemen of Washington
> Bicycle Federation of Washington
> Cascade Bicycle Club
> Iron Horse Covered Wagon Association
> John Wayne Pioneer Wagons and Riders
> The Mountaineers
> Transcontinental Trails Association
> Washington Trails Association

You can volunteer to build rail-trails. The Volunteers for Outdoor

Washington, The Mountaineers, Backcountry Horsemen of Washington, and the Backcountry Bicycle Trails Club all organize work parties for construction of rail-trails.

At the national level, the Rails-to-Trails Conservancy, a nonprofit advocacy group, began in 1984 to heighten public awareness of the value of rail-trails. This national organization has helped provide information to state and local organizations about rail-trails, has lobbied Congress on rail-trail issues, and has worked with the ICC on procedural issues.

Using Rail-Trails

A measure of the success of rail-trails is not just how many miles exist, but how people use them. One benefit of a rail-trail is that its surface is wide enough to accommodate several users at once. For example, the Burke-Gilman Trail in Seattle is very popular and has both paved and gravel surfaces that accommodate walkers, runners, bicyclists, and roller-bladers. Although the trail can be crowded at times, users have learned to follow the rules prescribed by the trail managers and to share the trail.

Trail Etiquette

One strength of rail-trails is that they can accommodate multiple uses. This increases support for their development by having a wider range of citizens involved. But it is the responsibility of all users to learn and practice sharing the trails so that rail-trails are safe and enjoyable for all.

In order for these uses to co-exist smoothly, it is important for users to follow proper trail rules and etiquette. No matter who uses these trails, there are some common safety and courtesy rules that will help make the multiple-use concept work. These include general rules that all trail users should follow, as well as specific suggestions for the more popular trail uses.

General rules

All trail users should observe the following rules:
- **Obey posted trail rules.**
- **Pick up litter.**
- **Keep to the right of the trail.**
- **Let other trail users know when you are passing.**
- **Report trail damage to the trail manager.**

- **Respect the rights of property owners adjacent to the trail.**
- *Do Not Cross Private Property!*
- **Stay on the trail surface.**
- **Do not create your own path to waterways or sensitive areas next to the trail.**
- **Do not disturb wildlife or livestock.**
- **Close all gates that you pass through.**
- **Be courteous to other trail users.**

Pedestrians/hikers

Many people enjoy walking, and rail-trails are an ideal place for a long or short walk. Pedestrians, like other multiple-use trail users, must take responsibility to share the trail. Just because their mode of travel is more basic does not give them any more inherent right in the use of the trail over any other users.

- **Do not cross through private property** to get to the trail.
- **Use the official trailheads** or signed access points.
- **Be aware of approaching bicycles and equestrians** and do not make abrupt movements across the trail.
- **On popular or crowded trails,** leave room for other users to pass safely.
- **Keep pets leashed** and clean up after your animal.

Bicyclists

Rail-trails are ideal for bicycling because they do not have tight corners and have gentle grades. Bicyclists generally go faster than other trail users and, because of this, they must use special precautions.

- **When overtaking another trail user,** slow down, announce that you are passing by ringing a bell or by calling out "passing on your left," and then pass on the left.
- **When approaching an oncoming bicyclist,** move over to the right of the trail as far as is safe and ride single file.
- **When approaching horses,** slow down, then make human noises such as talking, singing, or whistling. If requested by the horseback rider, dismount and move your bicycle away from the horse on the downhill side of any hill.
- **Be prepared** by keeping your bicycle in good repair and carrying equipment to make small repairs.
- **Always wear a helmet.**
- **Be sensitive to the earth;** walk through very soft or muddy areas and don't skid your rear tire.

Equestrians

Equestrians find rail-trails are one of the few public places they can take their horses for long rides. Where the trail surface is paved, many trail managers are providing separate equestrian trails. Equestrians must be careful to observe trail rules in order to remain welcome on many of the rail-trails both existing and under development.

- **Obey trail signs for equestrians;** use separate trailheads if available.
- **Don't take short cuts;** stay on the trail or on a separate designated equestrian trail if available.
- **Walk your horse across bridges** or steep grades.
- **Keep your horse under control** and at a walk around other trail users.
- **Announce your intention to pass.**
- **Let other trail users know** if your horse is safe to pass.
- **Stay out of soft, muddy areas.**

Other special users

In addition to being popular with walkers, bicyclists, and equestrians, rail-trails are also extremely popular with special types of users, including:

Families with strollers: Rail-trails are safe places for families with small children to take walks or ride bicycles.

Wheelchair users: Racers and motorized wheelchair users find rail-trails one of few places they can travel safely, yet be outside in a natural setting.

Race-walkers: Rail-trails provide a gentle grade and even surface for race-walking.

Roller-skaters: People on roller skates or roller skis enjoy having a paved path where there is a good, smooth surface and no cars.

Physically challenged: Because rail-trails are flat and often paved, people having difficulty walking due to age, disease, or injury find them a safe place to walk at their own speed.

Horse-drawn vehicle drivers: With the opening of the rail-trails in eastern Washington, horse-drawn wagons have been reborn in this state. Every year there is a wagon-train ride across the state, and the drivers find rail-trails to be perfect for their special needs. Drivers of horse-drawn sleighs also find them an ideal place to operate safely in the winter.

Cross-country skiers: Rail-trails are gently sloped and relatively safe from avalanches in the winter.

Sled-dog mushers: These outdoor enthusiasts enjoy an easy route to run their dogs.

How to Use This Book

At the beginning of this book is a map of Washington State showing the location of each rail-trail listed in the table of contents. In the back of the book is a listing by type of trail surface. The text description of each rail-trail includes the following information:

Trail name: Each trail description includes the official trail name if an official name exists. For those with no formal name, a name that describes the trail location has been used.

Trail manager: Included for each trail is the organization or agency that is responsible for managing the trail. The surface conditions, use restrictions, and degree of development of these trails are subject to change; so it is advisable to call or write the trail managers to get the most up-to-date information. A listing of the names, addresses, and phone numbers of trail managers is provided in Appendix 1.

Endpoints: The endpoints of a rail-trail are indicated using city names or an easily identifiable geographic point. Sometimes the railroad grade goes beyond these official endpoints of the open portion of a trail route. It is also possible that these trails will be extended in the future and the specified endpoints will change.

Length: The length of each rail-trail is indicated in miles for a one-way trip. The elevation gain or loss is not generally included because it is usually not significant.

Surface: There is considerable variation in the surface condition of rail-trails, from paved 10-to-12-foot-wide asphalt paths to original railroad beds of rock ballast. The surface also can vary over the entire route of a particular trail. The predominate type of surface fits within one of four categories: asphalt/concrete, hard-packed gravel, unimproved ballast, or dirt. While all the surfaces can be used by pedestrians, only the asphalt/concrete trails are suitable for road bikes—that is, bicycles with tires less than 1.5 inches in width. Even mountain bicyclists may find the loose gravel or unimproved ballast surfaces tough going. Equestrians may want to shy away from the asphalt or hard-packed gravel trails. Equestrians also should note that some ballast surfaces can be particularly hard on horses' hooves.

Restrictions: All the rail-trails listed in this book are closed to unauthorized motor-vehicle use except the Republic Rail-Trail. Included for each trail are restrictions made by the trail manager in terms of type of use and recommendations concerning which modes of travel may be difficult.

Original Railroad: The primary railroad company that built the original railroad is listed, as well as any other significant railroad history, such as the year of abandonment.

Location: The nearest city and the county are listed to help you identify the general trail location.

Description: There is considerable variation in the physical condition and ambience of these trails, from the concrete sidewalk of the Duwamish Bikeway to the wild, rugged natural terrain of the Milwaukee Road Corridor Trail. The description attempts to paint a verbal picture of each trail. Directions start from an interstate highway or a small community near the trail. These directions are to either the most popular trailhead or the one with the most parking. If appropriate, there is information on how to get to both ends of the trail and other good access points. Connections at both ends, intersections with other trails, and possible future links are noted.

Map: Included with each trail description is a map illustrating the entire route. This map shows roads, bodies of water, communities, and points of interest. For additional maps, call the trail manager listed at the top of each description (see Appendix 1 for addresses and phone numbers). Note that since many of these rail-trails are new, many do not appear on regular maps or show up as railroads.

A Note About Safety

Safety is an important concern in all outdoor activities. No guidebook can alert you to every hazard or anticipate the limitations of every reader. Therefore, the descriptions of roads, trails, routes, and natural features in this book are not representations that a particular place or excursion will be safe for your party. When you follow any of the routes described in this book, you assume responsibility for your own safety. Under normal conditions, such excursions require the usual attention to traffic, road and trail conditions, weather, terrain, the capabilities of your party, and other factors. Keeping informed on current conditions and exercising common sense are the keys to a safe, enjoyable outing.

Key to Map Symbols

Rail-trails ▬▬

Planned rail-trails ■ ▬ ▬ ■

Railroads ┼┼┼┼┼┼┼┼┼┼

Abandoned railroads ▦ ▦ ▦

Freeways ══════

State highways ───────

Streets/roads ─────

Rivers/lakes/bays 〜〜〜〜

Trails · · · · · · · · · ·

Mountain peaks △

Cliff ㅅㅅㅅ

Mountain pass ⟩⟨

Cities ●

Parks ▨▨▨

Former towns ✕

Buildings ■

Locations ▭

Northwest

Washington

1. Glacier—Maple Falls Trail
WHATCOM COUNTY PARKS AND RECREATION

Endpoints : Glacier to Maple Falls
Length : 8.0 miles
Surface : dirt/gravel
Restrictions : none
Original Railroad : Chicago, Milwaukee, St. Paul, and Pacific Railroad
Location : Glacier, Maple Falls, Whatcom County

This is an undeveloped rail-trail through the foothills of Mount Baker. While it is still in a rustic condition, it offers a deep-forest experience for explorers. This trail is the beginning of what will someday be the Bay to Baker Rail-Trail, which will extend from Bellingham Bay up to Silver Fir Campground, 70 miles east.

Before visiting this rail-trail, call Whatcom County Parks at (206) 733-2900. To get to the west trailhead, from I-5 take exit 255 (Sunset Drive) and go east on Mount Baker Highway (SR 542) to Maple Falls. In the woods behind the general store are the remnants of the grade. To get to the east end, continue east on SR 542 to the town of Glacier. The rail-trail begins just south and west of the general store and restaurant.

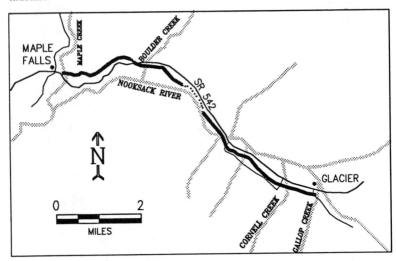

Maple Falls cascades deep in the woods

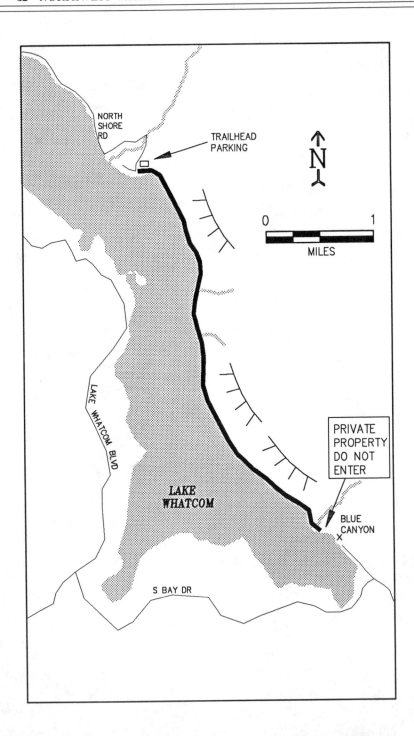

2. Lake Whatcom Trail
WHATCOM COUNTY PARKS AND RECREATION

Endpoints : North Shore Road to Blue Canyon
Length : 3.0 miles
Surface : gravel
Restrictions : none
Original Railroad : Lake Whatcom Railway
Location : Lake Whatcom, Whatcom County

This is a beautiful rail-trail alongside Lake Whatcom away from roads and houses. It skirts the lake beneath steep cliffs. The rail-trail was built in 1991, with many slides cleared and creek crossings improved. A unique feature of the trail is that it can be easily accessed via water.

To get to the west trailhead, take Lake Whatcom North Shore Road to its end (including the new, wide section going uphill from the lake). The road crosses a creek and heads back down to the lake, where you'll see a right-turn arrow. Take the first left and angle right into a small parking area.

The trail runs beneath steep cliffs with occasional waterfalls and several major stream crossings. The trail surface is only about 5 feet above the lake, and the water is always easily accessible. The sight and sound of the water is a wonderful feature of this peaceful trail.

Lake Whatcom laps against the trail.

The rail-trail currently dead-ends in 3 miles because of private property. DO NOT TRESPASS! You will be reported, cited and have to pay a hefty fine.

3. Old Robe Historic Trail

Endpoints : Mountain Loop Highway to tunnel 4
Length : 2.2 miles
Surface : dirt/rock, difficult footing in places
Restrictions : not recommended for bicycles or horses
Original Railroad : Everett and Monte Cristo Railroad, built 1893, abandoned 1936
Location : 10 miles east of Granite Falls, Snohomish County

Walk back in history to a rare place. This rail-trail follows the route of an historic railway instrumental in the Monte Cristo gold rush. Monte Cristo was a booming mining community deep in the mountains east of Everett at the headwaters of the Stillaguamish River. The railroad was the critical link in getting the ore from the mines around Monte Cristo to the smelters in Everett. The line ran from Hartford (near the modern community of Lake Stevens) to Monte Cristo at the head of the valley. Hiking this rail-trail, you will be awed by the tenacity of the men who carved the railroad down a steep river canyon. It was very difficult to build and almost more difficult to keep open. There were huge snowfalls that caused avalanches, and flooding tore out land underneath the rail bed and created landslides.

The rail-trail has a gentle grade, but the surface is as tough as the country it passes through. Be prepared for rough footing and, in places, steep drop-offs to the river. The land is so steep that tunnels were frequent along this route. Three of those tunnels are part of the experience on this rail-trail. You also can see how a roadbed was literally carved out of the bedrock alongside the river, with the troughs cut for ties still evident.

To get to the trailhead, take Mountain Loop Highway east of Granite Falls 7 miles east to the top of the long, steep hill. On the south side of the road (across from Forest Service Road 41) is a sign inscribed on a section of log marking the start of the Old Robe Historic Trail.

The trail starts out through a clearcut with high bushes, moves through deep trees, and joins the railroad grade in 0.2 mile. It moves out into a wide, flat bog area, the site of the original community of Robe. It remains smooth, wide, and flat until it joins the river at 0.7

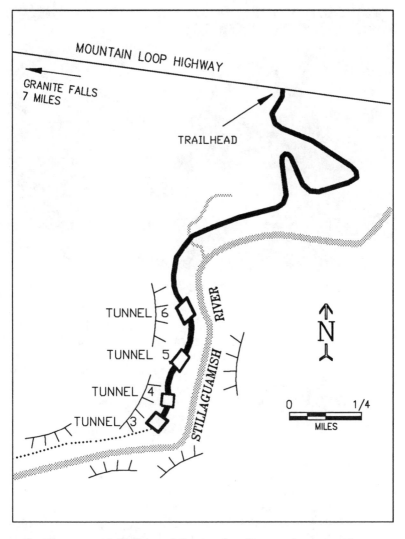

mile. Then steep hillsides and the results of years of erosion take over. There are several areas that are always wet, several stream crossings, and many rocky areas that require good balance and sure-footedness. If it's been raining recently, you also may have to walk through a small waterfall. This trail has not been improved except by the users.

At mile 1.2 you can see where the rock was chiseled out to hold the railway ties. The rock is preserved in the exact shape of the old ties just inches from the river gorge. Here the river gets very narrow and noisy, and the old railroad had to go through the hills to fit in the canyon. The

Railroad roadbed cut into the rock along the Stillaguamish River

first tunnel is at mile 1.4 and is called tunnel 6, the sixth tunnel from Hartford (now Lake Stevens), the start of the line. Tunnel 6 is about 250 feet long, on a slight curve, and with enough light even in the deep forest for claustrophobic visitors not to get nervous. At mile 1.7 is tunnel 5, 100 feet long and straight. Imagine carving these tunnels with hand tools! The next tunnel, number 4, was removed by the railroad and is now a cut with a rockslide at the west end.

Just beyond this point is a huge rock wall built up from the river to the grade. It served as the support for a wooden structure holding up the rails and prevented erosion by the river. Farther along is tunnel 3, which has collapsed.

Caution: The trail becomes dangerous beyond this point, and only those visitors experienced in off-trail scrambling should proceed.

One of the pleasures of this rail-trail is traveling next to the Stillaguamish River as it carves its way through a narrow canyon. It is very noisy as it plunges down through the canyon and you can hear the echo off the rock walls next to the trail. It is also easy to understand why the railroad was abandoned after many accidents caused by floods, avalanches, and slides.

Thanks go to the Boy Scout troop that made the trailhead sign and brushed the rail-trail. If you would like to experience more history, visit the Monte Cristo town site farther up the road. It is operated by the Monte Cristo Preservation Society and has a fascinating exhibit of old mining equipment and historical displays.

4. Port Angeles Urban Waterfront Trail
CITY OF PORT ANGELES PARKS AND RECREATION

Endpoints : Lincoln Street to ITT Rayonier Mill
Length : 5.8 miles
Surface : asphalt/gravel
Restrictions : none
Location : Port Angeles, Clallam County

This is a true waterfront trail with views everywhere. The rail-trail starts out at the vertex of waterfront congestion near the ferry terminal to Victoria and the city pier. There are shops, motels, and restaurants, as well as a viewing platform and sandy beach. After a few moments of walking on the trail, you are away from all the noise and congestion and can continue peacefully along the water's edge. This is an ideal place for a stroll, with views across the Strait of Juan de Fuca. It is also a popular place for short bike rides.

To find this rail-trail, go to Port Angeles and turn north on Lincoln Street to the waterfront (follow the signs for the Victoria ferry). The trailhead is at Lincoln Street and Railroad Avenue. There is also access at the north end of Francis Street.

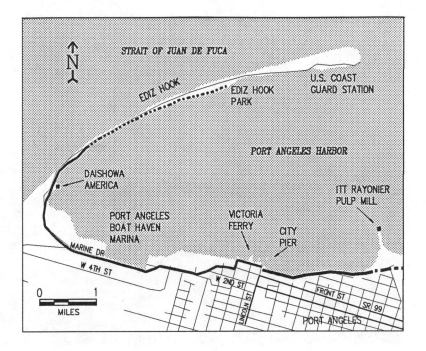

The rail-trail follows closely along the water's edge, barely 5 feet above the water at high tide. You are so close you can smell the salt air, hear the ferry whistles, and view the distant mountains of Vancouver Island. On a clear day you can even see the city of Victoria across the Strait of Juan de Fuca.

This rail-trail is very popular with local citizens on lunch breaks and with the numerous tourists who are waiting for the ferry or just exploring Port Angeles. The trail curves along the waterfront to the east, providing a good view back across the bay to Ediz Hook. It is always cool here, even on the hottest days, because the trail is sheltered from the sun by the steep hillside to the south and there is often a breeze blowing off the Strait of Juan de Fuca.

There are plans to develop this trail to the west. It will follow the waterfront along Railroad Avenue and Marine Drive west to the Daishowa mill and then all the way out Ediz Hook to Ediz Hook Park. There are also plans to extend the trail east to Morse Creek, adding another 4 miles on the waterfront. This trail will then provide a spectacular view of Port Angeles with the Olympic Mountains rising steeply to the south. Eventually the trail will be part of the Olympic Discovery Trail, which will connect Port Angeles and Port Townsend.

Walkers enjoy a clear day along Port Angeles harbor.

5. Railroad Bikeway

CITY OF BELLINGHAM PARKS AND RECREATION

Endpoints : Memorial Park to Lake Whatcom
Length : 4.0 miles
Surface : gravel/dirt
Restrictions : dogs on leash, no horses
Original Railroad : Bellingham Bay & Eastern Railway
Location : Bellingham, Whatcom County

This is a quiet neighborhood trail from central Bellingham to Lake Whatcom. It has a fine view west of Bellingham and the San Juan Islands and connects Memorial Park with Lake Whatcom Park. There is good wildlife viewing in the deep-forest area near Lake Whatcom, which includes several other trails, a dam, and a waterfall.

This trail is used a great deal for long walks by the people who live in the neighborhood. It is also a popular bike route, offering a safe, gentle, scenic route across Bellingham. Though the surface is not paved, it is usually suitable for skinny-tired bikes. The trail passes an elementary school and provides a safe route for children off busy streets.

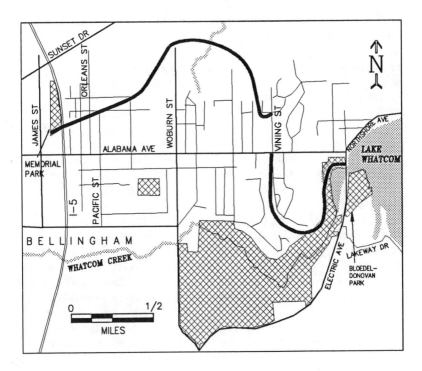

Young walkers alongside Scudder's Pond

To get to the west trailhead, take I-5 to exit 255 (Sunset Drive). Turn left (west) on Sunset Drive to James Street. Turn left (south) on James Street and left (east) on Maryland one block to King Street and Memorial Park. The trailhead is on King Street between North Street and Connecticut. To get to the east trailhead, park in the parking area at the intersection of Electric Street and Alabama Avenue at the west end of Lake Whatcom.

The trail starts at Memorial Park near I-5, crosses over an old railway span, and heads into a residential street. Because the railroad right-of-way is 100 feet wide, there is a buffer of shrubs and trees from most homes. The trail crosses a broad meadow and a small flood-control dam, with an opportunity for bird watching. Farther along, the route provides excellent views looking west over Bellingham to the San Juan Islands.

The gravel trail stops at Vining Street, but if you continue south along Vining you will connect with a section that goes through a new residential development. It then enters the deep woods of Bloedel-Donovan Park. This is a wonderful wooded area with a deep ravine and a substantial creek. There is a "Y" in the trail with the south spur leading to an old railroad trestle. Stay left (north) and you will come to Scudder's Pond. This small pond is named after the person who gave it to the city and is maintained by the North Cascades Audubon Society. It is home to many birds, and the trail alongside it has been improved by the local Audubon group. The rail-trail ends at Electric Street and

Alabama Avenue. Just across the street, on the shores of Lake Whatcom, an old steam engine is displayed on the park grounds.

6. Snohomish–Arlington Centennial Trail
SNOHOMISH COUNTY PARKS AND RECREATION

Endpoints : Snohomish to Edgecomb
Length : 14.5 miles
Surface : asphalt/gravel
Restrictions : none
Original Railroad : Seattle, Lake Shore & Eastern
Location : Snohomish to Edgecomb, Snohomish County

This is a wonderful rail-trail in the rural but growing part of Snohomish County. It provides a scenic route through an agricultural and forested section of the county that is fast becoming suburban.

The southern and northern halves of the trail are quite different. The southern portion, from Snohomish to Lake Stevens, is parallel to a two-lane arterial, paved, and in a shallow valley. The northern portion is unpaved, passes through woods and along a lake, and runs along a ridge, providing occasional views to the west.

To get to the south trailhead, take SR 2 to the Snohomish exit. Turn left onto Second Street and left (north) on Maple Avenue. Going north, the rail-trail will be on your right, about 1 mile north of town. The northern terminus of the paved portion of the trail is at 20th St. NE just east of Lake Stevens. The trail north of here is undeveloped and there is no public parking available where the trail intersects roads.

The trail starts in Snohomish, a long-time agricultural town that recently has seen tremendous growth. The old downtown area has many antique and food stores and is a wonderful place to start or end a trail journey. The trail starts at the north end of town alongside Maple Avenue. It parallels the Snohomish–Machias Road through lowland farm areas next to the Pilchuck River.

At Machias the trail lies away from the road and there is a trailhead. Where the trail crosses Division there is a small store on Machias Road. Going north, the trail is adjacent to Machias–Hartford Road and provides a safe route for nonmotorized users along a busy road.

The intersection with Hyland Road marks the location of the original community of Hartford. This is the site where the Monte Cristo Railroad branched off west up the Stillaguamish River.

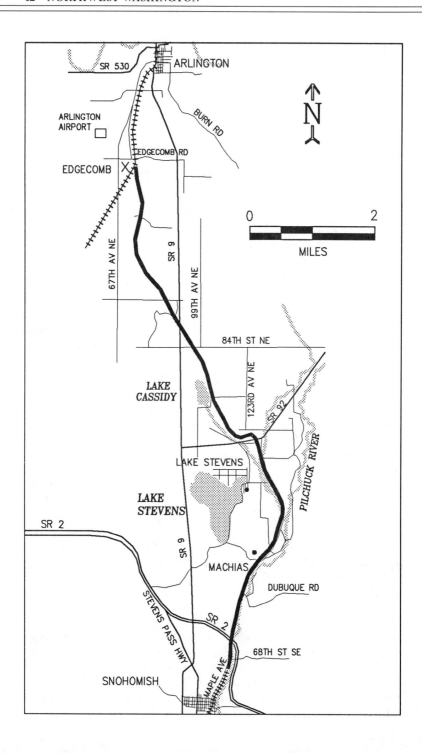

The crossing of SR 92 is a dangerous crossing, so please use caution. North of here the trail winds through a thicket of trees and alongside Lake Cassidy. There is a county park on the west side of Lake Cassidy, but the rest of the access is rather swampy. The trail traverses along a ridge above the land to the west, affording good views of the Olympic Mountains.

This trail is the result of the efforts of the Snohomish–Arlington Centennial Trail Coalition, a citizens' group that provided tremendous support to the Snohomish County Parks Department. The parks department plans to continue the trail north from Arlington on an abandoned line to connect with this trail if the active railroad is ever abandoned. There are also plans to connect it south through Monroe to the Snoqualmie Valley Trail in King County.

A group of equestrians near Lake Cassidy

7. Snoqualmie Pass Trail
WASHINGTON STATE PARKS
AND RECREATION COMMISSION

Endpoints : Cedar Falls to Hyak
Length : 22.0 miles
Surface : unimproved ballast/dirt
Restrictions : no hunting, no camping
Original Railroad : Chicago, Milwaukee, St. Paul, and Pacific Railroad
Location : Cedar Falls, King County

This rail-trail takes you into the mountains, literally! It includes a 2.25-mile tunnel through the Cascades and views of Mount Si, Bandera Mountain, Granite Mountain, Silver Peak, McClellan's Butte, Denny Peak, and the Tooth. The route parallels I-90 east of North Bend but has superior views and is cloaked in trees. The entire route is long enough for a full day of bicycling, and there are several access points for day hikes. It is also destined to become popular with equestrians.

The easiest access is from I-90 exit 38 and parking in the Twin Falls State Park parking lot. You also can access the rail-trail by taking the same exit and heading east to Forest Service Road 9020. Three other access points are the McClellan Butte Trail, the Annette Lake Trail, and the Hansen Creek Trestle. The west trailhead is near Rattlesnake Lake and the east trailhead is at Hyak.

To get to the western trailhead, take I-90 to exit 32 (436th Avenue SE). Turn right on Cedar Falls Road SE and proceed 3.5 miles. Just past Rattlesnake Lake (good swimming) is the former site of the Cedar Falls railway station, which has been dismantled and moved and is now a private home in Kent. Cross the first railroad grade and take the upper route on the left, going slightly uphill to the north and east. In the future, King County Parks will be developing a rail-trail from this point to North Bend and Snoqualmie Falls.

From the west trailhead at Cedar Falls, the trail skirts Cedar Butte, with 50-foot fir trees close on both sides. Starting at an elevation of 937 feet next to Rattlesnake Lake, the rail-trail gradually climbs at a steady 1.5 percent grade to 2,562 feet at the west portal of the Snoqualmie Tunnel. At about mile 3.0 is a small waterfall, and openings in the trees reveal views of Mount Si to the north. At mile 3.7 is a wide gravel area that is the site of the old Edgewick railroad station. At one point the trail is about 200 feet above the interstate and only about 0.25 mile away. It is very pleasant to be on a trail that parallels a major interstate but that is definitely separate and in the woods.

The trail is interrupted by a new power substation that was developed before the corridor became a trail. This power substation trans-

Crossing the Hansen Creek trestle

fers the electricity from a generating facility located underground at Twin Falls State Park. Just 100 yards east of the substation is the Twin Falls State Park trail that takes you down to scenic Twin Falls.

Continuing east, the rail-trail dead-ends 0.7 mile farther at the Hall Creek Trestle, where the middle span is missing. This was washed out in 1988 due to extensive clear-cut logging on the extremely steep slopes uphill. To avoid this dead-end drop-off, turn down the wide gravel road that leads to the exit 38 freeway interchange and the Twin Falls State Park parking area. It is about 5.5 miles to Rattlesnake Lake from this point.

Continuing east, there are two optional routes. There is a gravel road that goes south up Hall Creek under the missing trestle span for about 0.4 mile. Just upstream of the trestle there is a very steep and muddy trail up the left side of the creek that connects to the rail-trail. A less strenuous route is to continue up the old Snoqualmie Pass Highway 1 mile to Forest Service Road 9020 and continue 1 mile to where it crosses the grade at the old station stop called Garcia.

Another access point is via the McClellan Butte trailhead. This trail crosses the Snoqualmie Pass Trail at mile 13.1 and continues up to the top of McClellan Butte, another 3,700 feet above.

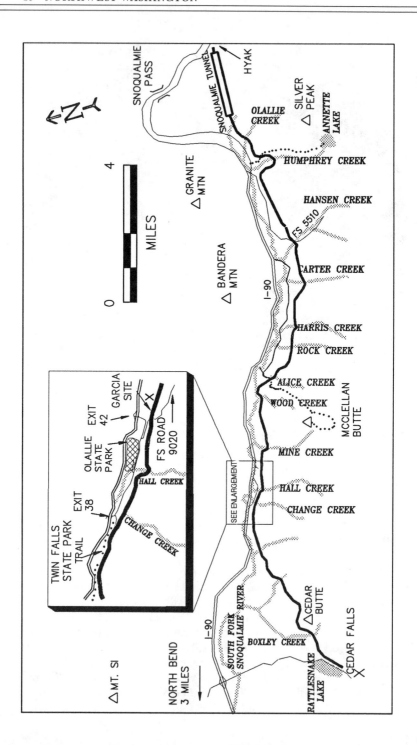

Hansen Creek Trestle, located at mile 18.7, is another access point and a place with spectacular views. This trestle is easy to identify because it is a very long, steel trestle on a curve with five overhead supports used to hold the electric lines that ran the train like an electric trolley. It is also covered with large, pink ballast rocks. There is access to this trestle from the Hansen Creek Forest Service Road 5510 off exit 45 from I-90. The access trail starts about 200 yards up the road from the trestle on the left (east) side. The first 50 feet are straight up, then it becomes easier. This access trail gains the railroad grade just beyond the east end of the trestle.

East from Hansen Creek is the Annette Lake Trail crossing. The Annette Lake trailhead parking is 0.5 mile downhill from this point. This trailhead can be reached by taking exit 47 from I-90.

Just east of the Annette Lake Trail crossing is an unusual trail structure: a wooden snowshed still in good condition. This snowshed is still doing its job of protecting winter travelers from the dangers of avalanches. Once you are east of the shed, look back above the shed and see the hilltop scoured of all large trees. The trail is generally well sheltered from avalanches for winter travel, but always check the weather reports. The best access during the winter is at the Garcia site via Forest Service Road 9020. This is a very steep road and you might have to ski or walk the last part.

The highlight of the trail is the Snoqualmie Tunnel, which was constructed between 1912 and 1914. It is 2.25 miles long and perfectly straight. The tunnel is probably still closed as you read this book, however. There is a large pair of wood doors at the eastern end at Hyak and a locked cyclone fence at the west end. The Forest Service owns the middle of the tunnel and refuses to allow the public passage through the tunnel until it has completed a safety inspection and made necessary repairs. It has not made any attempt to perform this work since it acquired the property in 1981. If you would like to see the tunnel opened, please contact the Forest Service and let them know of your interest. They have a similar tunnel under Stevens Pass which is open to the public and which was abandoned in 1910.

The east portal of the Snoqualmie Tunnel is at Hyak and can be reached by taking exit 54 (Hyak) from I-90, turning right, and immediately turning left on the frontage road toward the Washington Department of Transportation shops. The portal is at the intersection of the freeway exit and the entrance to the Hyak parking lot down in a cut. The tunnel is closed, however, with a pair of very large wooden doors blocking the entrance.

The Snoqualmie Pass Trail is a cooperative project of the Washington State Parks and Recreation Commission and the U.S. Forest Service, with the financial assistance of AT&T.

8. Snoqualmie Valley Trail
KING COUNTY PARKS

Endpoints : Duvall to Tokul Road
Length : 21.5 miles
Surface : gravel/dirt
Restrictions : none
Original Railroad : Chicago, Milwaukee, St. Paul, and Pacific Railroad
Location : Duvall, Carnation, King County

This is a wonderful trail through lush forests and the lowland farms along the east side of the Carnation Valley. The trail passes through the lowlands and climbs high enough to provide great views of the valley. It is an ideal place for equestrians, mountain bikers, hikers, bird watchers, and view seekers. It is very close to the urban Seattle area, yet is in a truly rural setting.

Adjacent to the trail near Carnation is a farm open to the public that has a restaurant, vegetable market, and a strawberry-picking festival in July. Both Carnation and Duvall are fast-growing small towns that offer good restaurants for the trail user.

To get to the north end of the trail, take SR 203 to Duvall. Immediately north of the bridge over the Snoqualmie River is an access road to the trail. To get to the south end, take SR 202 to Snoqualmie Falls. Turn north on Tokul Road 0.5 mile to a large culvert over the trail. Take the next side road to the right and look for a small trail down to the grade. The trail between Carnation and Duvall may not be improved so call the manager before going on this section.

The best access to the trail is in Carnation. This gives you the choice of going 9.7 miles south or 11.8 miles north one way. Take exit 22 from I-90, turn left (north) across the freeway, and turn right on the Preston–Fall City Road to Fall City. From Fall City, cross over the Snoqualmie River, turn left (northwest) on SR 203, and go 5 miles to Carnation. In the center of Carnation turn right on Entwhistle Street, go right (east) four blocks to Milwaukee Avenue, and park at Nick Loutsis Park. To get to the trail at Duvall, go down the steep road immediately north of the bridge over the Snoqualmie River.

Starting at Carnation, the trail begins at Nick Loutsis Park and heads south across the Tolt River Bridge. This is a very long bridge over the wide flood-plain area of the Tolt River, one of the water sources for Seattle. The trail passes behind Tolt High School and heads up and into the woods.

At 1.8 miles is a bridge over Griffin Creek with a beautiful view of the wide valley below. The trail is in second-growth woods with mostly deciduous trees covering the trail. Gradually the trail rounds a corner above Fall City, and through the trees you can see Fall City and Tiger Mountain in the distance. The current end of the trail is at Sparks

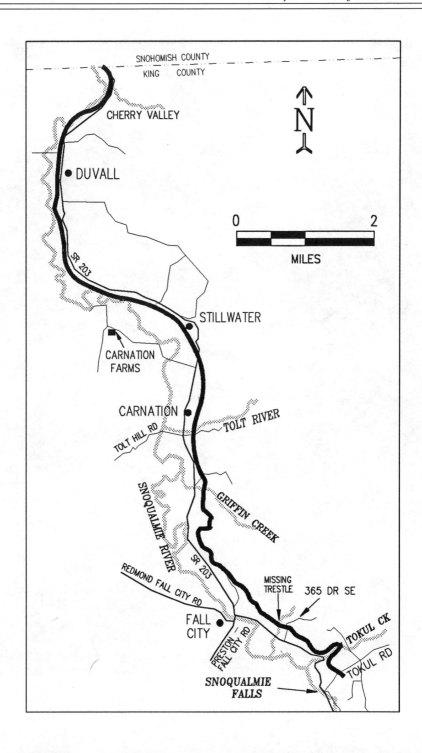

Horses and riders pause during a spring ride.

Creek, where King County Parks removed a trestle, creating a dangerous, impassable chasm.

To get to the next section of trail you must return to Carnation and take the road from Fall City to Snoqualmie Falls. Turn left on 356th Drive SE, proceed 2 miles east, and go uphill to the trail crossing. The trail east continues for 3.3 miles across the spectacular Tokul Creek Bridge and ends at an underpass of Tokul Road. This is 0.5 mile from the Snoqualmie Falls overlook.

Going north from Carnation the trail stays in the flat valley. Occasionally the Snoqualmie River meanders next to the trail grade. You'll find active farming and cattle ranching on both sides of the trail, and because the trail is elevated 10 feet above the valley floor you will have a great view.

In some places the fields are owned by the Department of Wildlife and are used for hunting in season. The access points have good parking areas near Stillwater, but you must have a Department of Wildlife Conservation license if you park a motor vehicle there. Because the railroad owned a 100-foot-wide right of way, there is a buffer of trees along this route between the trail and the surrounding farms. The trail currently ends at the growing community of Duvall, which has shops, restaurants, and a tack shop.

In the future this trail will continue north 3 miles to the Snohomish County line, where it will continue to Monroe. To the south, the trail will someday connect with a trail from Snoqualmie to Cedar Falls and to the Preston–Snoqualmie Trail.

9. South Bay Trail
CITY OF BELLINGHAM PARKS AND RECREATION

Endpoints :	Fairhaven to Bellingham
Length :	1.7 miles
Surface :	loose gravel
Restrictions :	none
Original Railroad :	Bellingham Bay & Eastern Railway
Location :	Bellingham, Whatcom County

This is a delightful trail that connects Fairhaven with downtown Bellingham via the waterfront. The trail has great views and passes through Boulevard Park on the water and near the Waterfront Park viewpoint. It is a popular trail for walking because of its outstanding views and the amenities of Fairhaven, Bellingham, and Boulevard Park. Mountain bicyclists will enjoy it as an interesting way to get between Bellingham and Fairhaven.

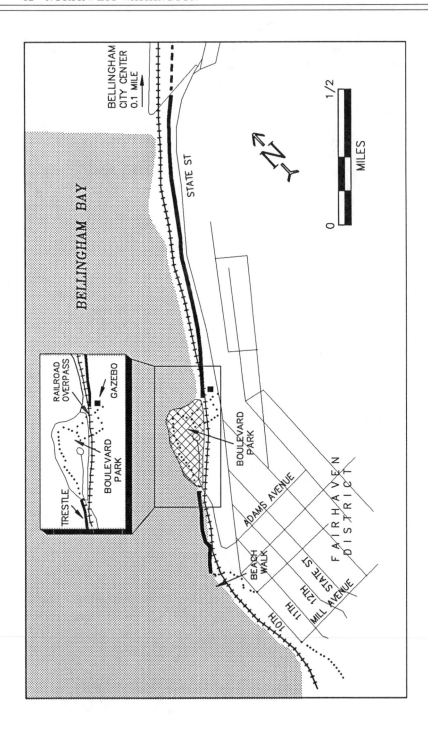

Fairhaven is a small community just south of downtown Bellingham that has been designated as a National Historic District. It has old, renovated buildings full of restaurants and shops. It is a fascinating place to visit at the start or finish of your trail trip.

To get to the southern trailhead, take I-5 to Bellingham and exit 250 (Old Fairhaven Parkway) into the Fairhaven District. Turn right onto State Street and left on Mill Avenue. The trail starts at the intersection of Tenth Street and Mill Avenue, although you can park anywhere in the Fairhaven District.

The gravel trail heads north and winds along the top of the cliff. In the future it will turn west out onto the public dock and go along the waterfront. In the interim it returns briefly to a quiet side street (Mill Avenue) and then heads steeply downhill and crosses the main-line Burlington Northern tracks. Use extreme caution when crossing these tracks as the trains are going very fast.

Part of the rail-trail is built over the water on the original pilings used by the railroad. This is a wonderful spot, especially for fishermen who sometimes crowd the walkway. The trail enters Boulevard Park, a large developed area with all the normal park amenities.

Heading north out of Boulevard Park you again must cross over the active Burlington Northern tracks. There is a beautiful wooden over-

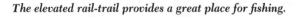

The elevated rail-trail provides a great place for fishing.

pass designed for pedestrian use, but it doesn't connect directly with the rail-trail. The route follows along the steep bank above the water and comes into the south end of downtown Bellingham. There is a side route uphill that connects with Waterfront Park, an overlook of Bellingham Bay. This area has a small shelter with a tremendous view of Bellingham Bay and the San Juan Islands.

Future plans will take this trail into the downtown area of Bellingham and connect it south to the Whatcom Interurban Trail.

10. Spruce Railroad Trail
OLYMPIC NATIONAL PARK

Endpoints : west trailhead to east trailhead
Length : 4.0 miles
Surface : dirt, rugged in places
Restrictions : no firearms, no pets
Original Railroad : Spruce Railroad, built 1918, abandoned 1954, trail opened 1982
Location : Lake Crescent, Clallam County

This is a delightful trail along the shores of beautiful Lake Crescent, so named because of its shape. It provides a great view and access to Lake Crescent, as well as a peaceful place to stroll. The trail is heavily used by hikers visiting Olympic National Park and is also ideal for mountain bikes. The trail was constructed in 1982 by the National Park Service.

The original railroad was constructed in 1918 in only five months by the U.S. Army from Port Angeles to 36 miles west. The reason for the hurry was that the Olympic Peninsula had one of the few good stands of spruce wood used in the construction of airplanes. In spite of the speedy work, World War I ended a few weeks before the railroad was completed. However, the railroad did haul logs for the next thirty years.

There is good access at both ends of this trail. To get to the east end, go west on Highway 101 from Port Angeles and turn north just before Lake Crescent onto East Beach Road. At 3.3 miles turn left and follow the signs to the Spruce Railroad Trail. To get to the west end, drive on Highway 101 past Lake Crescent and turn north on Camp David Jr. Road, the first road past the end of the lake. Stay left at the "Y" and go 4.9 miles to the end of the road and the trailhead.

The vegetation along the trail is not representative of the Olympic Peninsula. Because of the low elevation (580 feet), and being in a rain-

A bridge over a corner of Lake Crescent

shadow, parts of the trail are open forest with a different microclimate. There are species uncommon to the Olympics, including poison oak and madrone trees. This area is notorious for ticks, so take precautions.

The west end of the trail starts at the east end of a National Park Service parking area and goes up a short gravel path to the warning signs about poison oak and ticks. At both trailheads you'll find an informative brochure made available by the Pacific Northwest National Parks and Forests Association describing the history of the railroad with some excellent photographs.

At mile 1.0 the trail bypasses the 460-foot McFee Tunnel and drops down to the lake. There the National Park Service has built a steel-and-wood bridge across a short cliff area. The lake is so clear that you can

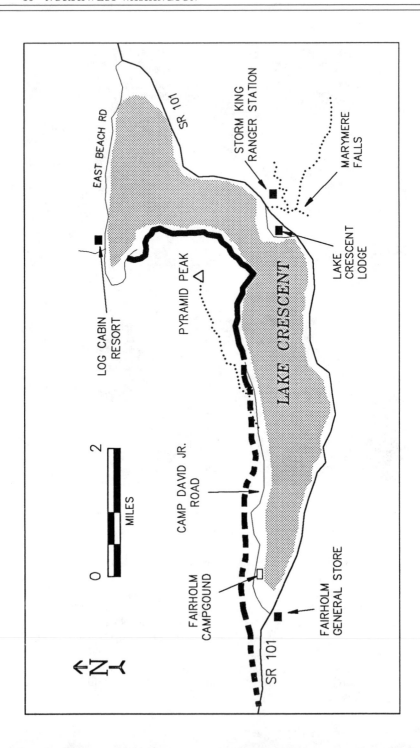

see more than 40 feet down into the light-blue waters. The lake is known for this clear water and its unknown depth. Across the lake to the south you can hear the rumbling logging trucks and see the Lake Crescent lodge. There is also an occasional motorboat.

The trail follows the old railway grade except where it passed through two tunnels. Generally the grade is wide, hard-packed dirt, showing the volume of use the trail receives. Be careful while circumventing the tunnels since the trail becomes more difficult, steep, and narrow.

Although the trail stops at the west end where Camp David Jr. Road ends, the railroad grade does not. Abandoned in 1954, the grade itself is in excellent shape and ready for continued use. It is hoped that someday this trail will continue farther west to Forks and perhaps east to Port Angeles and the Waterfront Trail.

11. Wallace Falls Railway Grade
WASHINGTON STATE PARKS
AND RECREATION COMMISSION

Endpoints : Wallace Falls State Park parking lot to footbridge
Length : 2.3 miles
Surface : dirt/gravel
Restrictions : no horses
Location : Gold Bar, Snohomish County

This is a delightful trail up an old logging railroad grade, which makes it steeper than most rail-trails. The canopy of trees is high, and there is always moisture in the lush underbrush and often on the trail. The trail is a well-worn route with many exposed rocks and is frequently wet or muddy. It is an alternative, parallel route to what is called the Woody Trail, which is open only to hikers.

To reach Wallace Falls State Park, take Highway 2 to Gold Bar and turn left at the brown sign indicating the park. Follow signs for 2 more miles to the parking area.

This is a cool place to go on a hot day. The trail is generally canopied with trees. You can still see the large, old stumps of the first logging in this area. Now most of the trees are deciduous. It is an area that gets a lot of rain, as witnessed by the abundance of moss and ferns. The park is extremely popular, so don't expect to be alone. The rail-trail is popular with mountain bicyclists, and there is a side rail-trail that goes an additional 7 miles up to Wallace Lake.

The trail starts at the parking lot of Wallace Falls State Park at an el-

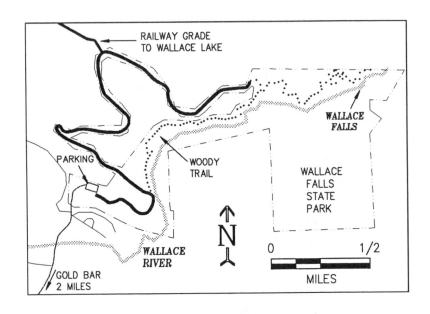

RAILWAY GRADE
TO WALLACE LAKE

WALLACE
FALLS

PARKING

WOODY
TRAIL

WALLACE
FALLS
STATE
PARK

N

WALLACE
RIVER

0   1/2

MILES

GOLD BAR
2 MILES

Families enjoy the wide, easy grade to Wallace Falls.

evation of 310 feet. It goes along a power line clear-cut area and then enters the deep woods. At 0.4 mile the rail-trail continues to the left and the Woody Trail goes right. At 1.5 miles there is another railroad grade that turns left to Wallace Lake (unsigned), about 7 miles farther. The DNR plans to make this old grade into a logging road soon. The rail-trail ends in 2.3 miles, and there is a short trail downhill that joins the Woody Trail.

Hikers can make a loop by hiking up the railway grade and down the Woody Trail. Hikers also can continue farther up the Woody Trail to the upper falls.

12. Whatcom County Interurban Trail
WHATCOM COUNTY PARKS AND RECREATION

Endpoints : Fairhaven to Larrabee State Park
Length : 5.5 miles
Surface : hard-packed gravel/dirt
Restrictions : none
Original Railway : Interurban Railway
Location : Fairhaven, Whatcom County

The Whatcom County Interurban Trail provides a wonderful alternative route to the ups and downs of Chuckanut Drive by providing a gentle, shaded grade. The rail-trail clings to the steep hillside above Chuckanut Drive, and the fact that the railroad grade is still there, while Chuckanut Drive continues to fall into the sea, is evidence of the good engineering and construction of the railroad. This rail-trail provides access to deep woods, creeks, and views of the San Juan Islands and connects to Larrabee State Park and the beach.

To reach the south trailhead, take Chuckanut Drive (SR 11) to Larrabee State Park. Go in the main entrance and park at the first parking lot. The trailhead and sign are directly across the road from the park entrance. The Fragrance Lake Trail (open only to hikers) starts from this parking lot and intersects the railroad grade in about 0.2 mile. The north trailhead is reached from I-5 by taking exit 250 (Chuckanut Drive, Old Fairhaven Parkway) and going 0.7 mile west on Old Fairhaven Parkway. Look for a large trail diagram sign on the south side of the road and park along the road.

Starting from the south, the trail begins in a canopy of second-growth and deciduous trees. The Fragrance Lake Trail turns off the Interurban at 0.2 mile and is for hikers only. There are a few places where private roads cross and use the rail-trail surface, but generally the trail lies in deep woods. In a couple of miles the view to the west opens up. Here the rail-trail is high on the hillside above the water with views out to the San Juan Islands. The canopy of trees makes it a wonderful place to be in the heat of the summer, and since most of the trees are deciduous, it is a wonderfully scenic place to be in fall. In the winter, the views to the west open up after the leaves have fallen.

Bicycling near Fairhaven

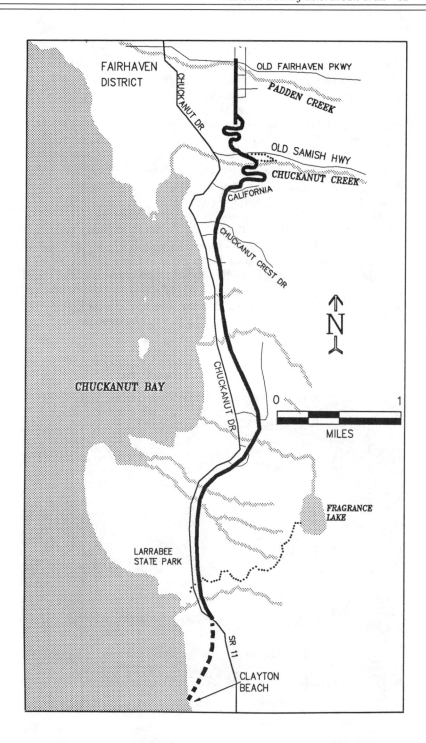

At 3.2 miles the trail crosses Chuckanut Crest Drive. The trail changes to a narrow, single track wandering between the trees and passes next to a small waterfall. The woods are very deep and dark here, even on a bright sunshiny day.

At 4.1 miles the trail enters Arroyo Park and crosses Padden Creek on a wooden bridge. There used to be a large trestle across the creek here, but now the trail winds steeply down into the creek bottom and across the low-level wood bridge before climbing up the opposite hillside. Take the trail leading downstream on the north side of the bridge; it will take you up to Old Samish Highway. This is a beautiful creek drainage heavily covered with tall trees.

At 4.6 miles the trail passes out of Arroyo Park and crosses Old Samish Highway. On the north side of Old Samish Highway you'll find the site of an old trestle foundation and a bench to sit on. The trail opens up again to a 10-foot-wide dirt path. It enters a residential area, although it is hard to tell since the trailside vegetation acts as a visual barrier. The trail ends at 5.5 miles at the north trailhead on Old Fairhaven Parkway. There is no parking lot, but you can park along the road. To get to Fairhaven via a road, go five blocks west to Chuckanut Drive and turn right.

A short life for a railroad, now reborn as a rail-trail

There is also an informal trail to Fairhaven from the north trail-head. Go west along Old Fairhaven Parkway to 16th Street and turn south to a small parking area. The gravel path leads down into the woods along Padden Creek. Going downstream, the trail passes under Chuckanut Drive and comes out on Donovan Avenue. Continue west on Donovan Avenue to Tenth Street and turn right. Go straight two blocks to Fairhaven and four blocks to reach the South Bay Trail. Bellingham Parks has plans to improve the informal trail and South Bay Trail in the future.

This trail gets heavy use from the residents of Bellingham. It has many access points, so pedestrians can get on it easily. It is very popular with runners, and several 10K races are held on it every year. Mountain bicyclists find the trail ideal since it leads to numerous trails in the hills above Larrabee State Park.

At the south end, there is a good connection to Clayton Beach at Larrabee State Park. Although not officially developed yet, the Clayton Beach Trail is a wonderful route to the beach from the Larrabee State Park trailhead. Clayton Beach Trail is the southward extension of the Interurban right-of-way. You'll find a parking area on Chuckanut Drive. The trail is not in good shape—there is a creek running down the center of it—but State Parks has plans to upgrade it. The highlight of this trail is that it leads right down to the beach.

This rail-trail is a result of the cooperative efforts of Whatcom County Parks, State Parks, and Puget Power and Light and is a wonderful addition to the Bellingham area trail system.

Puget

Sound

13. Burke-Gilman Trail
CITY OF SEATTLE ENGINEERING DEPARTMENT, KING COUNTY PARKS

Endpoints : Eighth Avenue NW to Sammamish Slough
Length : 15.2 miles
Surface : 8-foot asphalt; gravel path alongside part way
Restrictions : no horses, 15-mph speed limit, dogs on leash
Original Railroad : Seattle, Lake Shore & Eastern Railroad, abandoned 1971, trail opened 1976
Location : Seattle, King County

The Burke-Gilman Trail is one of the oldest and most popular rail-trails in the United States and a wonderful example of an urban rail-trail. It is located on the abandoned railroad grade of the Seattle, Lake Shore & Eastern Railroad, which was started by Judge Thomas Burke and Daniel Gilman in 1885 to haul goods and passengers around Lake Washington. It is a preferred bicycle commuting route also used by walkers, recreational bicyclists, roller-skaters, runners, race-walkers, wheelchair users, and even mothers on roller-blades pushing large-wheeled baby carriages.

The trail is extremely popular with bicyclists, who comprise more than 80 percent of all trail users. It makes a wonderful bypass of the hilly and busy Lake City Way and is an excellent route to get around the north end of Lake Washington since bicycles are excluded from the Evergreen Point Floating Bridge. Young children first learning to ride bicycles and adults looking for exercise will both find this rail-trail ideal.

The numerous access points and dense population along the entire route is one reason the Burke-Gilman Trail is so popular, although half the users drive to get to the trail. The trail has become so popular with nearby neighbors that many have constructed small, informal access trails from their property to the trail.

There are four parks bordering the route: Gasworks Park, Matthews Beach Park, Tracey Owen Station, and Blyth Park. These make great destinations or picnic stops, but the rail-trail itself is also a park that traverses steep ravines and creeks and often passes under canopies of trees. It is a cool place on hot days and provides shelter from the wind on stormy days.

Although the trail extends west to Eighth Avenue NW, the most popular trailhead is at Gasworks Park at the north end of Lake Union in Wallingford. Take I-5 to exit 169 (45th Street); turn west to Stoneway Avenue N and then south (left) onto Stoneway Avenue N. Proceed to the bottom of the hill and turn left on Boat Street, continuing east four blocks to Gasworks Park.

The east end of the Burke-Gilman Trail lies at the west end of the Sammamish Slough Trail in Bothell. From I-5, take Lake City Way (exit 171, SR 522) to Bothell and turn right on NE 180th Street in Bothell. Park at the Bothell Landing Park. The Sammamish Slough Trail lies across the arched bridge over the slough and connects with the Burke-Gilman where the railroad trestle passes over the slough.

Gasworks Park is the site of an old power-generating facility that developed electricity by burning coal taken from the Newcastle mines and barged across Lake Washington from the present-day Newport area of Bellevue. It is also the site of another rail-trail (see Puget Sound: Coal Creek Park Trail). Gasworks Park has a spectacular view of Seattle and Lake Union with its crowded boat traffic, water access, and great kite flying. You can watch power boats, sailboat races (called the Duck Dodge because of the crowded conditions) on Tuesdays in the summer, float-planes departing for points north, and kite fliers on windy days.

From Gasworks Park it is about 1 mile to where the trail passes through the University District, crossing "The Ave" (University Way). This is an area with shops, restaurants, and the changing flavor of a university. Between the University Way and 15th Avenue crossings is a small park, adjacent to the trail, named the Bob Pyle Wilderness after

Great views of downtown Seattle and Union Bay

a University of Washington student who became famous as a butterfly expert.

The trail is extremely popular with university students and staff for commuting, walking through campus, and exercising. The trail passes the Hec Edmundson Pavilion and Husky Stadium, where a footbridge spans busy Montlake Boulevard NE. This footbridge is the safest bicycle route for those going south over Montlake Bridge. There are mileage markers beginning from Gasworks Park and a variety of mileage markers beginning at the overpass near the Hec Edmundson Pavilion on the University of Washington campus.

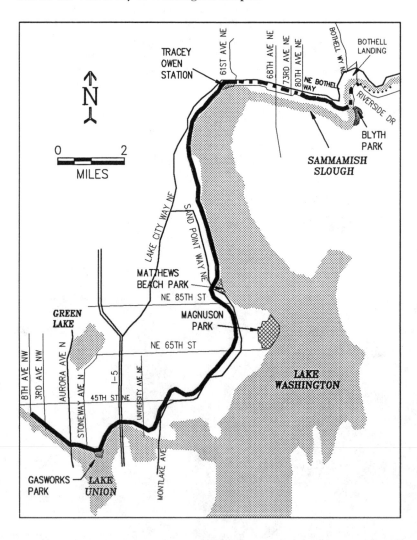

Where the trail crosses 40th Avenue NE there is the small Burke-Gilman Park, with a playground, picnic benches, and a creek alongside it. Beyond this point the trail enters deep woods and divides for a short distance into two one-way lanes. There is also a gravel path on one and sometimes both sides of the paved surface that is especially popular with runners.

Magnuson Park is a large natural area on Lake Washington with a swimming beach, boat launch, tennis courts, and restrooms. It can be accessed by leaving the trail at the NE 65th Street crossing and going downhill across Sand Point Way NE.

At mile 7.1 the trail skirts Matthews Beach Park. This is the last public access to Lake Washington for several miles. This park has restrooms, playgrounds for small children, picnic tables, and a shallow, sandy beach.

The trail passes through a residential area with narrow private-access paths. You can get glimpses of Lake Washington between and over the tops of houses. At mile 10.0 the trail leaves the Seattle city limits and is under the jurisdiction of King County.

At mile 11.9 is a side trail to Tracey Owen Station, a small park next to the water. There are restrooms, picnic tables, bike racks, water access via a sandy beach, ducks, and a view of Lake Washington.

The next mile has been called the "Missing Link" because, when completed, it will link the Burke-Gilman Trail with the Sammamish Slough Trail. It should be completed by the time you read this. If not, take NE 175th Street east, cross 68th Avenue NE (Juanita Drive), and turn back onto the rail-trail at 80th Avenue NE.

At mile 14.5 there is a tunnel under 96th Avenue NE. Beyond this point there is a trail going left to Bothell Landing, a City of Bothell park on the Sammamish Slough. The rail-trail may someday continue across the Sammamish Slough on an old railway trestle through Blyth Park to 102nd Avenue NE. Either route connects with the Sammamish Slough Trail for an additional 12 miles to Redmond.

Because of the high volume of use and variety of users there is the potential for overcrowding and user conflicts. The trail managers have posted signs and trail rules that have helped reduce problems. Trail users generally follow the rules, with bicyclists calling out "On your left" or ringing a bell when passing. The trail is patrolled on mountain bikes by the City of Seattle Police and Animal Control officers.

The Burke-Gilman Trail is a valuable asset to Seattle. When part of it was almost lost to an out-of-town developer, the outcry was incredible. The entire city rallied to prevent the loss of even an inch of the trail and to support further expansion. This popularity will ensure that the Burke-Gilman Trail will continue to be a treasure to Seattle and an outstanding example of the value of developing urban rail-trails.

14. Coal Creek Park Trail
KING COUNTY PARKS

Endpoints : Newcastle Road to meadow
Length : 1.5 miles
Surface : dirt/gravel
Restrictions : no horses or bicycles
Original Railroad : Seattle and Walla Walla Railroad, built 1878
Location : west side of Cougar Mountain, King County

The history of the coal era in Puget Sound lies buried along this trail with some relics of the past still visible. The Newcastle town site was the terminus of the Seattle and Walla Walla Railroad, which hauled coal from the Newcastle mines to the wharfs of Seattle. It is a quiet place for a walk in a historic location. The trail is located in the upper reaches of Coal Creek, aptly named after the rich coal-producing area from which it flows.

To find the east trailhead, take the Coal Creek Boulevard exit from I-405 and proceed east to Newcastle Road. Turn left (north) on New-castle Road to where it crosses Coal Creek (a tight corner). Park in the parking area for Cougar Mountain County Park and cross Newcastle Road. Go across a small meadow and look for a sign (on a tree) marked "Elizabeth's Trail."

Along the trail you will find wooden signs—erected by the Boy Scouts with King County Parks assistance—that will help you under-stand the history of this area. On the south side of the creek is the site of the coal dumps, where coal was loaded from mine cars onto main-line railroad cars. There is also evidence of the shoring used to build over the creek, and there are still some artifacts in the bushes.

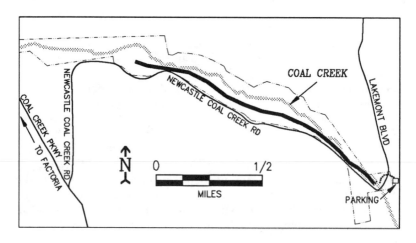

A gentle waterfall along Coal Creek

The trail heads west, gradually deteriorates in a broad meadow, and is blocked by private property in about 1.5 miles. King County Parks owns the land farther down in the creek valley, and it is possible to follow the creek for another mile.

The trail is located in a King County Park, although it has not been well developed. An interpretive center for relics collected by the Newcastle Historical Society would be a useful addition.

15. Corridor Trail
CITY OF SNOQUALMIE PARKS BOARD

Endpoints : Bruce Street in Snoqualmie to Snoqualmie River
Length : 0.4 mile
Surface : asphalt
Restrictions : no horses, dogs on leash
Original Railroad : Seattle, Lake Shore & Eastern Railroad, built 1890, trail opened 1989
Location : Snoqualmie, King County

This is a rail-trail for steam railroad fans. The trail is constructed alongside an active railroad, with scenic train excursions operated by the Snoqualmie and Puget Sound Railway. A nonprofit group has beau-

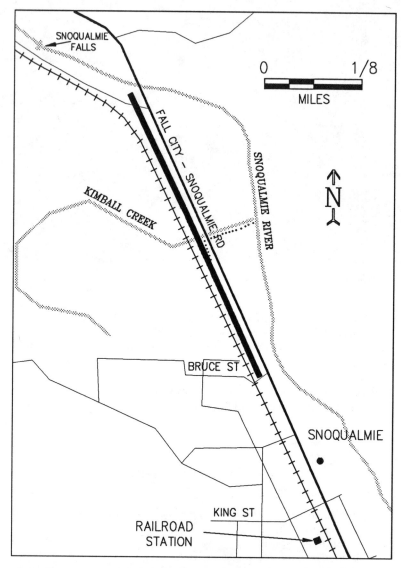

tifully restored the train depot, steam engines, and many railroad cars. Excursion trains run on summer weekends and for Halloween and Christmas. This trail also serves as a safe route for nonmotorized use between Snoqualmie and Snoqualmie Falls, avoiding the narrow and busy Highway 202.

The Seattle, Lake Shore & Eastern Railroad was built by Daniel Gilman, one of the partners who built the railroad route along which the Burke-Gilman Trail is now located. This railroad originally opened from Seattle as far as Snoqualmie Falls on the Fourth of July in 1890.

To get to the trail, take I-90 to exit 31 and follow SR 202 through North Bend to the center of Snoqualmie. Park just west of the railway station on the south side of the railroad tracks. The trail starts farther west at Bruce Street and is served by Metro buses 210, 211, and 213.

The trail crosses Kimball Creek where there is a new footbridge. There is also a narrow dirt path that goes north under Highway 202 and leads to the Snoqualmie River, where there is a great view of Mount Si. The trail ends at the intersection of Highway 202 and the Snoqualmie River. Stay on the sidewalk across the bridge and then you can walk through a parking area to get to Snoqualmie Falls. You'll also find access to the Snoqualmie Valley Trail by going north on Tokul Road for 0.5 mile.

The trail connects to the east with a sidewalk system on the south side of the parking lot that goes to the Snoqualmie Railway Station. In the future, King County Parks plans to extend its Preston–Snoqualmie Trail up to Snoqualmie Falls.

The steam engines still operate at Snoqualmie.

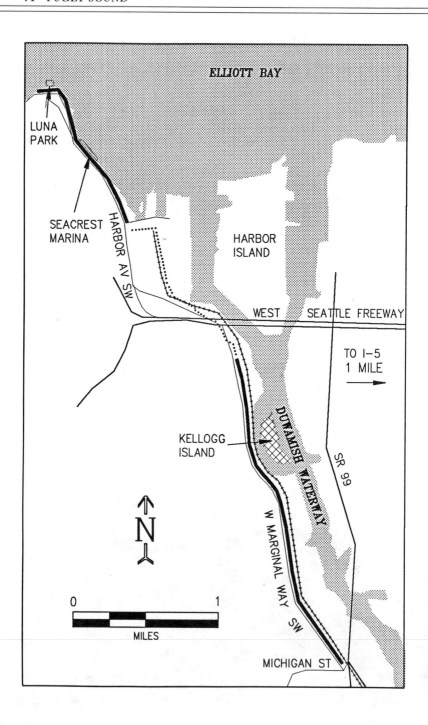

16. Duwamish Bikeway
CITY OF SEATTLE ENGINEERING DEPARTMENT

Endpoints : Luna Park to Michigan Street
Length : 4.8 miles
Surface : asphalt/concrete
Restrictions : none
Original Railroad : Seattle & San Francisco Railway & Navigation Co.,
built 1903
Location : West Seattle, King County

Views, views, views! This is a wonderful spot for looking at Puget Sound, the Olympic Mountains, and downtown Seattle. The trail is really a sidewalk alongside Elliott Bay and the Duwamish River with good access to several public parks. There are many nearby amenities, including food, fishing, and water access. Stop at the Seacrest Boat House for fishing information, aquarium displays, and quick lunches.

This trail is ideal for walks with family or out-of-town visitors. It is also popular with roller-skaters, roller-bladers, and bicyclists on their way to Alki. The views are spectacular. The Olympic Mountains are so close, with what looks like only a small body of water separating the viewer from their snowcapped peaks. There is always a variety of boat traffic on Puget Sound and Elliott Bay. The trail offers perhaps the best view of Seattle's skyline, with the Space Needle and Smith Tower acting as bookends for the numerous skyscrapers.

To get to the north end of the trail, take the Spokane Street bridge to the Harbor Avenue exit and go north to where Harbor Avenue turns west. This landform is called Duwamish Head because it is the head-

The Seattle skyline provides a wonderful scene for walkers.

land next to the outflow of the Duwamish River. The trail starts at Luna Park, the small park on the bay side of Harbor Avenue. To get to the south end, take I-5 to the Michigan Street exit. Go west to West Marginal Way SW, the southern terminus.

The trail officially starts at Luna Park at the start of the Alki Drive Bikeway. Just south is a large park, popular with fishermen, with a boat launch and restrooms. Farther south is Seacrest Marina, which has a large fishing dock, small fishing boats to rent, and a shop with fishing supplies and a soup-and-sandwich deli.

At Florida Street the trail ends, but you'll find a bike route along Florida Street to West Marginal Way SW. Go east on Florida Street to West Marginal Way SW and follow it under the West Seattle Freeway. There is a paved bike path on the south side of this street going under the freeway.

The rail-trail begins again at SW Dakota Street. The Burlington Northern railroad is still active, and the trail is wedged between the railroad and neighboring businesses. While not particularly scenic here, the trail does provide a safe, nonmotorized route along a busy road with much truck traffic. There is access to Kellogg Island, a wildlife sanctuary, but primarily the trail parallels West Marginal Way SW and the railroad. This is an example of how an active railroad right-of-way can be shared for nonmotorized use, providing the only route through an otherwise very developed area.

The trail connects west with the Alki Drive Bikeway, which runs all the way to the point at Alki. The City of Seattle plans to continue this trail south to Tukwila.

17. Franklin-Kummer Trail
WASHINGTON STATE PARKS
AND RECREATION COMMISSION

Endpoints : Franklin Bridge to SR 169
Length : 2.5 miles
Surface : dirt/gravel
Restrictions : none
Original Railroad : Columbia and Puget Sound Railroad
Location : 4 miles southwest of Black Diamond, King County

This rail-trail is located in Hanging Gardens State Park, which is undeveloped and very scenic, with dense second-growth timber. You'll find relics from the mining around Black Diamond, an old mine shaft, and a very old cemetery, and hear the sound of the Green River far below.

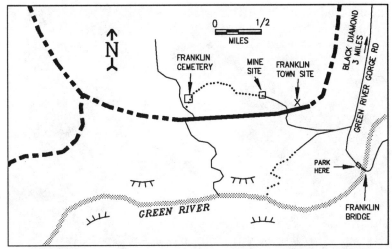

To get to the trailhead from Black Diamond, head east on Green River Gorge Road. Stop when you reach Franklin Bridge, which spans the gorge; it is closed to motor-vehicle traffic due to structural decay. Park along the road near the bridge. The obvious grassy parking area on the north side of the bridge is private land. However, from the entrance of this private land to the white gate on the east edge of the state park is a county road right-of-way. The railway grade starts at the west end of the parking area beyond the white gate.

This rail-trail has not been improved except for portions that are used as a roadway. It's short enough to be good for hiking, but mountain bicyclists also have enough area to test their muscles, especially if they go down to the river. Equestrians should take the high route through the cemetery to avoid a steep washout across a creek on the lower railway grade.

The road at the parking area leads uphill and crosses the railway grade at 0.3 mile. To the right of this point is the town site of Franklin, once a busy mining town; all that remains are several concrete foundations, a mine shaft, and the railroad grade. Continuing uphill on the road takes you out of the entrance to an open, vertical mine shaft (covered to keep people out). The rail-trail goes left (west) at the intersection with the road. There is one washout area across a creek that makes for difficult footing.

In about a mile the rail-trail becomes a good gravel road used as an access road by the City of Black Diamond to get to their water-supply pumping station. The side road that heads downhill from this point drops to the Green River and is steep, losing about 500 feet in elevation. Just above this intersection is an old cemetery. If you look around

An old gravestone in the Franklin cemetery

you can find many headstones completely covered by vegetation, including some dating back to the late 1800s.

If you continue to the west you will walk along the old railroad bed that is graded for use as a road. DANGER! Be forewarned that you are downrange of a popular gun range. You will come to a tight corner in the road that was a "Y" for the railroad. The narrow path to the right is the main line to Black Diamond but is private property. The road continues to the left for 0.5 mile to a white gate, then heads out to SR 169 in another 0.5 mile.

You might notice that the ground is black where the railroad used to operate. The years of coal spilling off rail cars have left their mark. If you look around carefully you can still find large chunks of coal, old cables, foundations, and even a small trestle used for mining cars.

This rail-trail is part of Hanging Gardens State Park, an undeveloped state park property. In the future a rail-trail might be developed that would link Franklin through Black Diamond and Maple Valley to Renton.

18. Issaquah Creek Trail
KING COUNTY PARKS

Endpoints : High Point to Issaquah
Length : 2.0 miles
Surface : hard-packed gravel
Restrictions : no camping
Original Railroad : Seattle, Lake Shore & Eastern Railroad, built 1890
Location : High Point, 2 miles east of Issaquah, King County

This rail-trail offers an easy hike/bike route in a beautiful forest alongside Issaquah Creek. Though very close to an urban community and freeway, it is a safe, secluded, tree-lined rail-trail. The trail is a wonderful place to unwind after work and in the hot summer is relatively cool with its cover of trees. It is great for walking, mountain biking, and horseback riding. It is also uncrowded compared to the hordes that regularly park across the freeway at the Tiger Mountain trailhead.

To get to the east trailhead, take I-90 to exit 22 (High Point) and

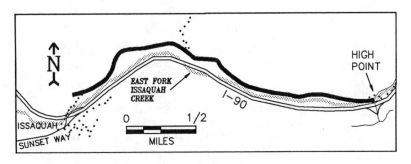

Mountain bikers enjoy the easy grade.

turn north under the freeway just past the interchange to a parking area west of the frontage road. Metro Bus 210 has a stop here.

This rail-trail parallels I-90 just east of Issaquah. The trail connects to the west with Issaquah. However, you must leave the railway grade and duck under the freeway where Issaquah Creek goes under I-90. Going east from High Point there is a faint trail between the creek and the freeway fence all the way to the Preston–Snoqualmie Trail.

19. Issaquah Trail
CITY OF ISSAQUAH PARKS AND RECREATION

Endpoints : train depot to Gilman Boulevard
Length : 0.7 mile
Surface : concrete
Restrictions : none
Original Railroad : Seattle, Lake Shore & Eastern Railroad, built 1890
Location : downtown Issaquah, King County

This rail-trail runs alongside an operating railroad. The trail is a concrete sidewalk that connects the restored train depot to the Gilman Boulevard sidewalk system. It complements the reconstruction of the railway depot and connects with the local city park. The trail offers a

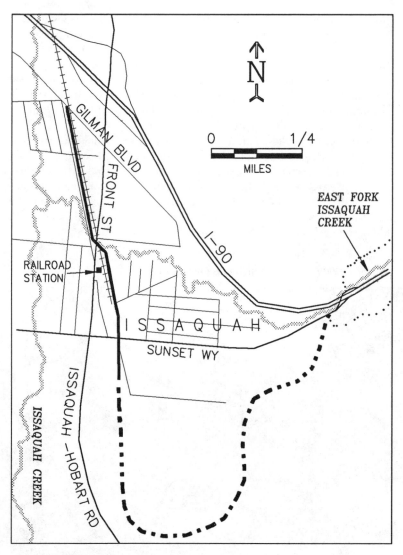

good place for walking in the center of Issaquah and a safe bicycle route to Gilman Boulevard.

To get to the trail, take I-90 to exit 15, the Issaquah Front Street exit. Drive up Front Street to Sunset Way, turn left, and proceed two blocks. You'll find parking near the city park on the left or in the open gravel area to the right.

The trail connects the new growth area of Issaquah, Gilman Boulevard, with the old town center. It goes past a dairy processing plant, the last shipper still using this active railroad line, which goes to Redmond. To the south of Front Street the line is not active but is used by the Issaquah Historical Society to store old railroad cars next to the refurbished railway station. This station is a museum worth seeing.

Downtown Issaquah is a National Historic District and many old buildings have been restored. The rail-trail makes it enjoyable to walk through the area. There are many shops and food establishments in the area and several public facilities.

For a less developed trail, continue south and follow the right-of-way as it curves around in a big half-circle and comes out at Sunset Way. The City of Issaquah plans to improve this trail in the future. Carefully cross Sunset Way and look for a small way-trail that heads under the freeway and connects to the Issaquah Creek Trail. When the railroad leaves, King County Parks plans to continue this trail north along the east side of Lake Sammamish to Redmond.

The beautifully restored Issaquah railway station

20. King County Interurban Trail
KING COUNTY PARKS,
CITY OF KENT PARKS AND RECREATION DEPARTMENT

Endpoints : Tukwila to Pacific
Length : 13.6 miles
Surface : asphalt
Restrictions : open in daylight only
Original Railroad : Pacific Traction Company, abandoned 1929
Location : Tukwila, Kent, Auburn, Algona, Pacific, all in King County

Cutting through the midst of a forest of warehouses in the Kent Valley is a path of green. The King County Interurban Trail follows the route of the old interurban railroad that once connected the urban centers of western Washington. Where the route once served as a major transportation corridor through farmland, it now serves as a major recreation corridor through industrial development. This rail-trail was made possible because Puget Power and Light purchased the right-of-way for a high-voltage power line that runs the entire trail length.

This rail-trail offers a long route for a quiet bike ride or walk away from busy streets, with views of Mount Rainier and, along the southern half, what is left of the green farmlands of the Kent Valley. It is one of the oldest rail-trails in Washington State, with parts of it opened in 1972, and exemplifies how preserving a railroad right-of-way for a trail also preserves greenspace. Since the construction of this trail, most of the Kent Valley has been taken over by major warehouse buildings, but this trail preserves a strip of green right down the middle of the valley. It also preserves small wetland strips and provides food and shelter for a variety of animals, including birds, rabbits, frogs, and numerous insects.

The trail is also popular with wheelchair users, particularly wheelchair racers, who regularly train here. These athletes have a special need for long stretches of paved surface safe from motor-vehicle traffic. One local company makes special racing chairs that you may see being used on the trail.

Though there are areas with concrete tilt-up buildings on both sides, the trail is somewhat quiet because it is isolated from most motorized traffic by those same buildings. The route parallels the Union Pacific's active main line, which comes as close as 30 feet at times. There is no real danger since sufficient green marshes exist to keep people from the tracks, and the passing trains remind trail users that trains once ran where they now walk, run, and bicycle. The trail is popular with those who work in the Kent Valley. Many use the trail for their commute and even more use it for daytime exercise.

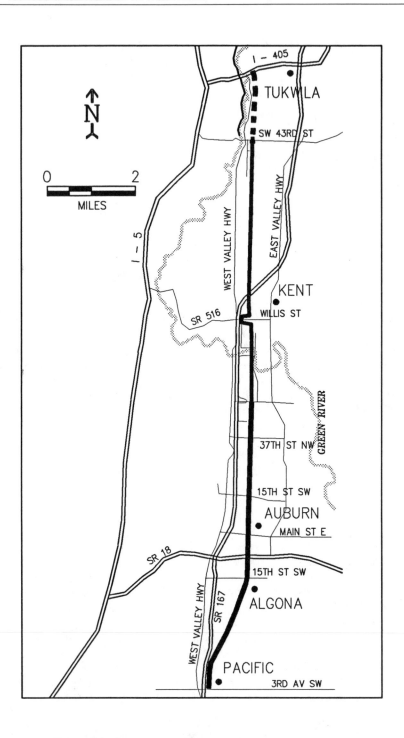

I – 405

TUKWLA

SW 43RD ST

EAST VALLEY HWY

WEST VALLEY HWY

I – 5

N

0   2
MILES

SR 516

KENT

WILLIS ST

GREEN RIVER

37TH ST NW

15TH ST SW

AUBURN

MAIN ST E

SR 18

15TH ST SW

WEST VALLEY HWY

SR 167

ALGONA

PACIFIC

3RD AV SW

A thread of green in an industrial area of the Kent Valley

To get to the north end of the trail, take I-5 to I-405 and go east to West Valley Highway. Go south to SW 43rd Street (also signed S 180th Street). Turn east two blocks, turn south one block on 72nd Avenue S, and take the first left onto 182nd Street. The trail is directly east. The section north of here to Tukwila is unpaved. At the north end of the trail you can connect with the Christensen Greenbelt Park by going west on SW 43rd Street just across the Green River and taking an immediate turn north along the riverbank. The trail goes north to Tukwila and eventually follows the Duwamish River to Alki. To get to the south end of the trail, take Highway 167 to the Algona exit. Turn east under Highway 167 one block and go south to Pacific. Turn left on Third Avenue SW one block and you'll find a parking lot on the north side of the street adjacent to the trail.

Starting from the north end, the trail winds alongside the very large power transmission towers. On the west are the backs of large warehouses. On the east is a border of green and then the mainline railroad tracks with an occasional train. The trail goes four miles south with little interruption until it passes under SR 167 and skirts the east side of the Kent Uplands Playfield. The old downtown of Kent is three blocks east. There you can find food, shops, and baseball diamonds. A farmers' market is held off Smith Street on the second Saturday during the summer months.

The rail-trail winds west to cross Willis Street, a main east-west arterial through Kent. It then regains the railroad grade and goes south one mile to a new bridge over the Green River. There is a small park just north of this bridge with picnic tables adjacent to the river. The bridge provides a good view of the water and the trains crossing the railroad trestle only 100 feet to the west.

Continuing south the trail crosses two railroad spurs to large automobile storage areas. It then crosses 74th Avenue S and goes across a smaller bridge over a wetland area. There are a few parking spaces just north across 74th Avenue S.

The trail south is separated from most of the industrial buildings and offers views of working farms, old barns, occasionally Mount Rainier, and airplanes landing at the Auburn Airport. At mile 10.0 is the Auburn trailhead on NW 15th Street with parking for about twenty cars. At mile 12.5 cross First Avenue N in Algona, where you can find a restaurant and minimart near the trail and parking for trail users. The southern terminus of the trail is at mile 13.6 in the town of Pacific at Third Avenue SW near Highway 167, with parking for ten vehicles. The railroad grade south of here lies in Pierce County and has not been developed yet.

21. Lake Wilderness Trail
KING COUNTY PARKS

Endpoints : Maple Valley to Summit
Length : 3.9 miles
Surface : hard-packed dirt/loose gravel
Restrictions : none
Original Railroad : Columbia and Puget Sound Railway
Location : Lake Wilderness, King County

This is a short section of what will someday be a longer rail-trail running from Maple Valley to the Green River. The current opened section extends from Lake Wilderness County Park north to Maple Valley and south to Summit. An interesting feature of this trail is that the dirt surface is very black, the result of years of coal falling off the trains used to haul coal from Black Diamond.

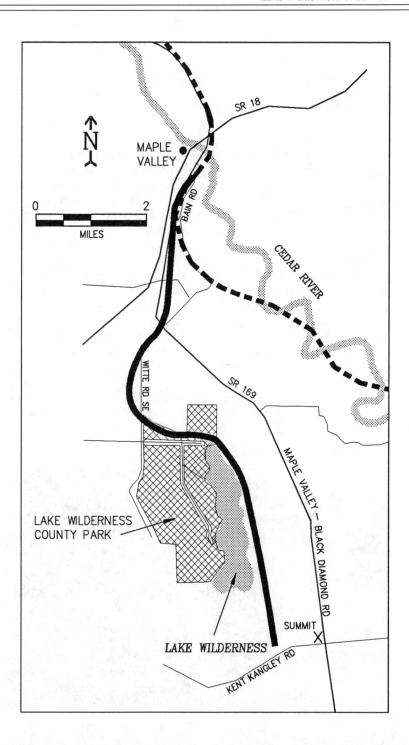

The best access to the trail is via Lake Wilderness County Park. It is about 2 miles in each direction from Lake Wilderness County Park to the current trail ends. The park is located next to a large lake with a swimming beach, boat rentals, and a conference facility. Take SR 169 to Witte Road SE and turn right (south) at the Lake Wilderness sign. At 0.8 mile turn left (east) to Lake Wilderness County Park. The rail-trail is across the lake. Follow the paved path at the northeast corner of the parking area to the back of the conference center and take one of several small paths heading east into the woods. To get to the north end of the trail, take the Maple Valley highway (SR 169) to Maple Valley. Cross the Cedar River, then take the first left (Bain Road) and park in the gravel area. The trail is at the top of a steep hill next to the highway. To get to the south end, take Maple Valley–Black Diamond Road to the intersection with Kent Kangley Road. The trail begins behind the shopping area to the northwest of the intersection.

This trail is ideal for hiking and long enough for a good workout on a mountain bike. While it is open to horses, some of the trail surface to the north of Lake Wilderness County Park is rocky and parts are brushy. Most of the time the trail lies in a cut, with no views and sometimes a rocky surface. Nearer Maple Valley it is overgrown with bushes and blackberries in the fall. Going south, the trail passes through a new housing project and ends in the back of a new shopping center near Summit.

Just north of the conference building by the lake is an arboretum developed by the South King County Arboretum Foundation. It in-

Overlooking Lake Wilderness

cludes a wonderful series of trails that crisscross the rail-trail in deep, dark woods.

The name "Lake Wilderness County Park" may seem incongruous today with all the growth in the area. While at one time this county park may have been viewed as wilderness, housing now encroaches upon the lake. For example, on the east side of Lake Wilderness, the rail-trail runs right through the middle of a new development.

King County plans to improve this trail in the future and connect it at Maple Valley with a trail running from Renton to Snoqualmie. There are also plans to extend the trail south to Black Diamond and eventually to Flaming Geyser State Park.

22. Laughing Jacob's Creek Trail
KING COUNTY PARKS

Endpoints : East Lake Sammamish Parkway to 42nd Avenue
Length : 1.6 miles
Surface : dirt/gravel
Restrictions : none
Location : 2 miles north of Issaquah, King County

This is a wonderful rail-trail in an undeveloped canyon with waterfalls. Although modern urban development is taking place on all sides, this trail exists in a garden of green. It provides a gentle pathway between Lake Sammamish and the Sammamish Plateau.

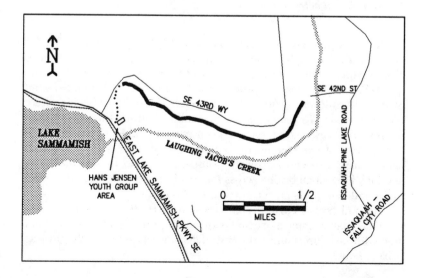

A waterfall deep in the woods

To get to the east trailhead, take exit 17 (Issaquah) from I-90. Go north on East Lake Sammamish Way and turn right on the first arterial, Issaquah–Fall City Road. Go up the hill and turn left on Issaquah–Pine Lake Road and proceed for 1.6 miles. Turn left on SE 42nd Street and continue to the end of the road. The rail-trail begins where the road ends. To get to the west trailhead, from East Lake Sammamish Way turn right (east) at the entrance to the Hans Jensen Youth Group Area of Lake Sammamish State Park, just across from the boat launch area. Proceed across the campground field toward the creek and look for a small bridge across the creek. Follow the footpath uphill to the railroad grade on the north side of the creek.

The rail-trail is currently an access road for the sewer utility but someday may become a pristine pathway. It provides a beautiful, quiet area with lush forest and large waterfalls very close to rapidly growing urban sprawl.

23. Myrtle Edwards Park Trail
CITY OF SEATTLE ENGINEERING DEPARTMENT

Endpoints : Pier 70 to Pier 89
Length : 1.25 miles
Surface : 8-to-10-foot-wide asphalt
Restrictions : separate paths for pedestrians and wheeled vehicles, pet scoop law
Original Railroad : Seattle, Lake Shore & Eastern Railroad
Location : Seattle waterfront, King County

This trail is situated at the water's edge in the City of Seattle with a stunning view across Puget Sound to the Olympic Mountains. It is so close to downtown that hundreds of runners parade through Myrtle Edwards Park during their lunch hour. There is a strange contrast in hearing the sounds of the city and the lap of the waves against the breakwater; of seeing the city skyline and smelling the salty air off the seawater.

This trail is very popular with walkers and runners. It is also a major commuting route for bicyclists on their way to work downtown. The separate walking and wheeled-vehicle paths help greatly during the busy summer months.

To reach the southern access, go to Alaskan Way on the Seattle waterfront and go north to Broad Street. The park entrance is at the intersection of Broad and Alaskan Way. To reach the north access, drive down Elliott Avenue W to W Galer Street and turn west toward the water. The right lane is marked to the Pier 89 public fishing pier. There is good parking at both ends of the trail.

The trail starts at the south end near the trolley maintenance shops. The trolley is a recent addition to the Seattle waterfront and runs south to Pioneer Square. The trail is actually two pathways: one for bicycles and one for pedestrians. The pedestrian path is closer to the water and passes various pieces of public art. Just over the fence to the east is an active Burlington Northern switchyard, which holds cars serving the large grain terminal. This terminal has an interpretive sign next to the trail explaining its operation.

This trail provides views in all directions. To the south you see the towering Seattle skyline, the busy waterfront, and the huge cranes of the port facilities. To the west you look across Elliott Bay to Alki and beyond the Olympic Mountains. To the north you see the steep bluffs of Magnolia. Overhead is a constant stream of planes for both the Sea-Tac and Boeing fields. There is a variety of boat traffic on Elliott Bay, including cruise liners, commercial ships, tugs, the ever-present ferries, and the occasional Coast Guard icebreaker or military vessel.

Approximately 1 mile from the south end is a large, modern public

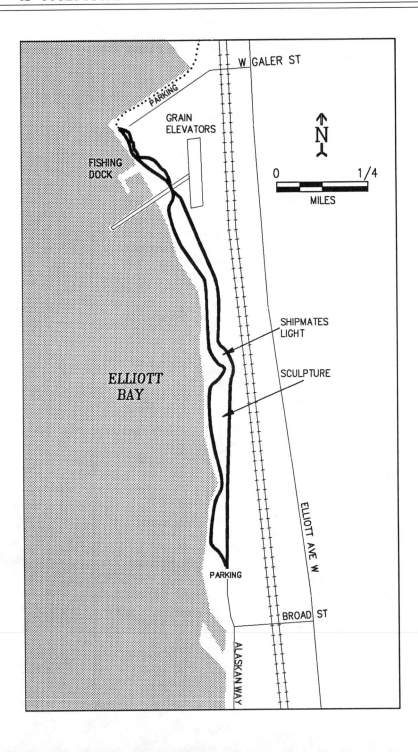

Running is a popular activity along the Seattle waterfront.

fishing dock with a bait-and-tackle shop open in the summertime. You can come down and catch dinner off the dock, and many people do.

Near the north end of the park is a par course, an exercise course running along the park. For those more interested in views than exercise, there are many park benches along the route and ample views.

Although commonly referred to as Myrtle Edwards Park, the northern part of the park is Port of Seattle property and is called Elliott Bay Park. This park was opened in 1975.

At the north end, the trail leaves the waterfront and proceeds alongside a parking area. It connects with the Terminal 91 Bike Trail accessed at W Galer Street. At the south end, there is a connection with the sidewalk system along the waterfront and Alaskan Way, and perhaps someday a connection with the Seattle Waterfront Path.

The restored North Bend railway station

24. North Bend–Tanner Trail
CITY OF NORTH BEND, KING COUNTY PARKS

Endpoints : Railroad depot to Tanner Road
Length : 2.5 miles
Surface : gravel
Restrictions : none
Original Railroad : Seattle, Lake Shore & Eastern Railroad, built 1890, trail opened 1989
Location : North Bend, King County

This rail-trail has superb up-close views of Mount Si from the town of North Bend. It runs from the restored railway station in North Bend east to Tanner. Although the trail parallels a main two-lane highway running east from North Bend, most of the traffic is local since the freeway has siphoned off the high-volume traffic.

To get to the west trailhead, take exit 31 from I-90 and head north to town. Just after crossing the railroad tracks, turn right onto SE North Bend Way and turn right again in two blocks into the parking area. The trail begins at the railway depot and heads east. There is no formal parking place at the east end at Tanner.

The trail begins at the depot in William Henry Taylor Railroad Park. The restored depot serves many community functions. The Puget Sound & Snoqualmie Railroad runs from the town of Snoqualmie to North Bend and back in the summer (see Puget Sound: Corridor Trail).

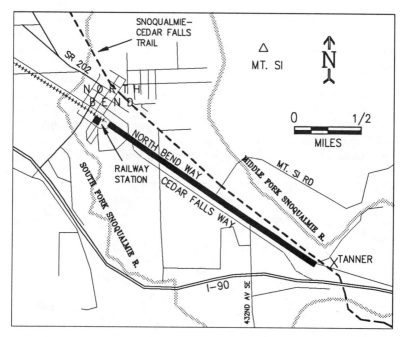

This trail is used mostly by the local community for exercise and as a safe place to walk or ride a bike next to the highway. The first several hundred yards are paved and then the surface is gravel out to Tanner.

Someday the trail will connect with the proposed Snoqualmie–Cedar Falls Trail at Tanner, a project of King County Parks.

25. Preston Railroad Trail
DEPARTMENT OF NATURAL RESOURCES

Endpoints : Crossover Road 5500 to Main Tiger Mountain Road 4000
Length : 5.0 miles
Surface : dirt
Restrictions : none
Original Railroad : Preston Railroad, abandoned 1920s
Location : Tiger Mountain State Forest, King County

High on the east side of Tiger Mountain is a wonderful rail-trail built on an old logging railroad grade. The existence of the railroad grade provides a strong foundation for a variety of nonmotorized uses. It also makes the construction of this trail far easier than other trails.

One of the unique features of this trail is that it provides a fairly gentle route nearly to the top of a 3,000-foot peak with a tremendous view. The entire trail is in deep woods, which keep it cool in the summertime and protect people from gentle rains.

To get to the lower end, take SR 18 to Tiger Summit. You can ride or walk the power line downhill to the eastside road, or park at its intersection with SR 18, although this will someday be blocked. Follow the eastside road northeast 4.2 miles to a switchback. Turn uphill on the Crossover Road 5500 for 300 feet and look for the trail entrance on the uphill side. To get to the upper end of the trail from Tiger Summit,

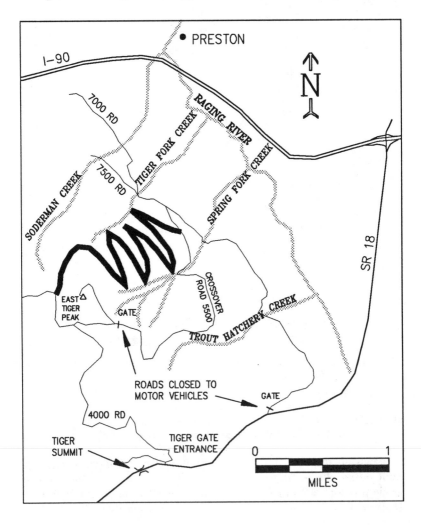

take the Main Tiger Mountain Road 4000 2.5 miles to the first intersection. Turn left and proceed 200 yards to a low spot in the road. The trail is to the right, at the base of the steep hill.

This trail was built by volunteers through the coordination of the Backcountry Bicycle Trails Club. It is an example of a user group working cooperatively with the managing agency and other user groups to create a well-designed trail.

Laurie and Bill have fun in the woods.

26. Preston–Snoqualmie Trail
KING COUNTY PARKS

Endpoints : Preston to Snoqualmie Falls overlook
Length : 6.2 miles
Surface : asphalt with gravel switchbacks
Restrictions : 15-mph speed limit, dogs on leash
Original Railroad : Seattle, Lake Shore & Eastern Railroad, built 1890, abandoned 1974, trail opened 1978
Location : Preston, King County

This is a paved rail-trail that wanders along through deep woods and emerges with a spectacular view of Snoqualmie Falls. Most of the trail is in second-growth timber with deciduous trees. This makes it cool in the summer and allows for views during the winter. Part of the trail is ten years old; yet it still does not receive a great deal of use.

The trail is good for walking any time of the year. The pavement ensures dry feet, even in the rain, and it is almost never covered with snow. It also makes a good bike ride, although there is one section of gravel switchbacks that presents a challenge even for the skilled mountain-bike rider. Equestrians are welcome, although the paved surface may not be to their liking.

To get to the main trailhead at the western end, take exit 22 (Preston) from I-90 and head north across the freeway. Turn immediately right on the Preston–Fall City Road for two blocks and turn left on SE 87th Place. There is a small parking lot for seven cars.

One part of the trail continues west from the trailhead 0.9 mile through an industrial area and then ends. Going east, the trail goes above the town of Preston, an old (and still current) mill town. It traverses the hillside north of town where there is a wide path down to the town site and to Preston County Park. The trail continues along a steep hillside until it comes to where there used to be a tremendous trestle across the valley of the Raging River. It descends very steeply to the Preston–Fall City Road and then climbs gravel switchbacks up to the original grade. At the top of the switchbacks is a bench, along with views back across the valley.

At 3.5 miles from the Preston trailhead you'll find a parking area and trailhead at Lake Alice Road; then the trail continues to a beautiful overlook of Snoqualmie Falls at 5.3 miles. Though you are about 2 miles away, you can see the falls and the lodge hanging over the lip, and in the spring you can hear the thunder of the cascading water.

A spectacular view of Mount Si and Snoqualmie Falls

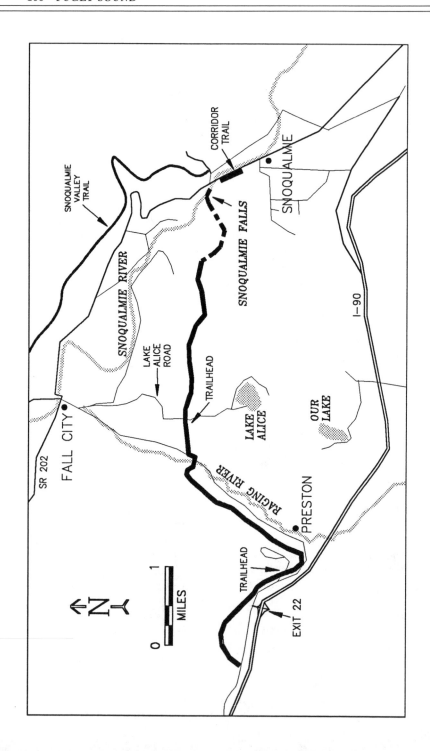

From the western terminus there is no formal trail heading west. Bicyclists can use the frontage road to High Point to connect with the Issaquah Creek Trail. Hikers can follow the faint trail along the freeway fence that eventually leads to the Issaquah Creek Trail. In the future this trail may continue east to Snoqualmie Falls with an even more spectacular view than the current trail.

27. Seattle Waterfront Pathway
CITY OF SEATTLE ENGINEERING DEPARTMENT

Endpoints : South Main Street to Pike Street
Length : 0.6 mile
Surface : asphalt
Restrictions : no horses
Original Railroad : Seattle, Lake Shore & Eastern Railroad, trail opened 1990
Location : Seattle waterfront, King County

This is a unique rail-trail that was created to improve pedestrian movement in the waterfront area of Seattle. For years the railroad tracks and the Alaskan Way Viaduct were a barrier to pedestrians passing from downtown Seattle to the waterfront. The City of Seattle reclaimed one of its most valuable assets, the waterfront area, and this trail improves the nonmotorized access. The trail was developed between a new trolley system and the Alaskan Way Viaduct, creating a nonmotorized corridor in a heavily used area of the city.

To reach the trail, go to downtown Seattle and Alaskan Way on the waterfront. The rail-trail lies immediately east of the trolley tracks between Main and Pike. It is used mostly by pedestrians but also is appropriate for low-speed cyclists trying to avoid narrow and busy Alaskan Way.

At the south end of the trail across Alaskan Way is the Washington Street Public Boat Landing and a small park. Farther north is the Washington State ferry terminal, with ferries to Bainbridge Island and Bremerton. There are trolley stations every two blocks; these offer an alternative method to return to your starting point.

The trail currently ends near the Pike Place Hillclimb. This is a pedestrian route to get to the Pike Place Market, perched high on the hillside. The market has a variety of fresh food and fish vendors, small shops, and restaurants.

The City of Seattle plans to continue this rail-trail north almost to

the Myrtle Edwards Park Trail. There is also the possibility of a bike route continuing south along Alaskan Way and crossing the Duwamish River.

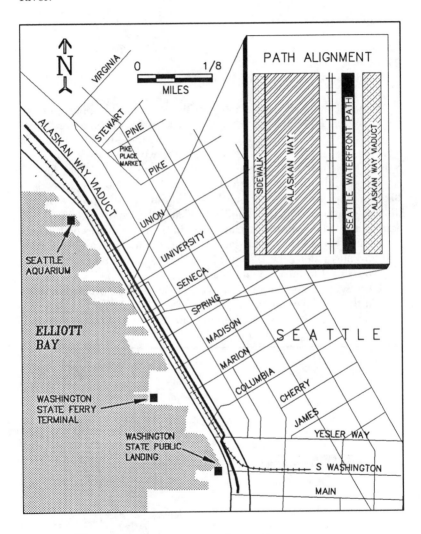

A rail-trail amidst the crowded Seattle waterfront

28. Sylvia Creek Trail
WASHINGTON STATE PARKS
AND RECREATION COMMISSION

Endpoints : Lake Sylvia
Length : 2.3 miles
Surface : dirt/gravel
Restrictions : none
Location : Montesano, Grays Harbor County

Two rail-trails, old and new, provide a wonderful opportunity to see beautiful Lake Sylvia, Sylvia Creek, and the surrounding forest. The old route follows the railroad grade along the edge of the lake. A new extension has been carved through the woods downstream along Sylvia Creek in order to show visitors the activities in a working forest.

To get to the trailhead, turn off SR 12 at Montesano and go north to the first stoplight. Turn left and then right onto Third Avenue. Go uphill and continue straight 1.5 miles to Lake Sylvia State Park. Turn left across the bridge over the lake and park in the parking area on the left. There are two rail-trails that start from this point. The older trail goes east and north along the lake and is called the 2-mile trail. The newer trail starts next to the dam and heads downstream.

Lake Sylvia State Park is located on a beautiful lake created by a log dam in the early days of logging in the area. The land for the park was donated by the City of Montesano to State Parks in 1936, and the park

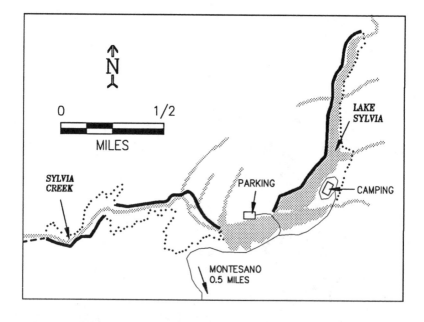

The old railroad bridge provides a great place for fishing.

continues to be very popular, with a swimming area, camping, and trails.

The new trail is a project of the City of Montesano with the assistance of the DNR. There are plans to extend this trail down to Simpson Street in Montesano.

29. West Tiger Mountain Railroad Grade
DEPARTMENT OF NATURAL RESOURCES

Endpoints : Tiger Mountain Trail to Poo Poo Point Trail
Length : 4.0 miles
Surface : dirt
Restrictions : foot travel only
Original Railroad : High Point Lumber Company
Location : Issaquah, King County

Tiger Mountain State Park has numerous trails carved upward to Tiger Mountain's summits. This rail-trail provides an easier route with little elevation gain, although you must climb 1,350 feet in elevation to get to it. The rail-trail lies on the grade of one of the numerous railroad grades that crisscross the Tiger Mountain area. This area was originally logged in the early part of the century, using railroads for access, before roads were common.

To get to the trailhead, take I-90 to exit 20 (High Point). Turn right and right again onto the frontage road and proceed to the Tiger Mountain State Forest parking area. Take the main trail uphill. Where the trees open up under a power line, take Tradition Lake Trail to the left. Stay on this trail as it climbs, with one trail going left and a second (Section Line Trail) going right. The trail gets steeper and crosses the railroad grade at about 1,800 feet. The trail right (west) contours around the mountain about 3 miles to the west side road. The trail going left (east) is quite well used to where it intersects Tiger Mountain Trail. To the east of this point the railroad grade is less worn and finally disappears into a creekbed in about 0.5 mile.

There are several loops possible with this rail-trail. The Department of Natural Resources has a good map at the High Point parking area. You can make loops using the Section Line Trail, Poo Poo Point

A stump from the 1920s shows the notch cut for the springboard.

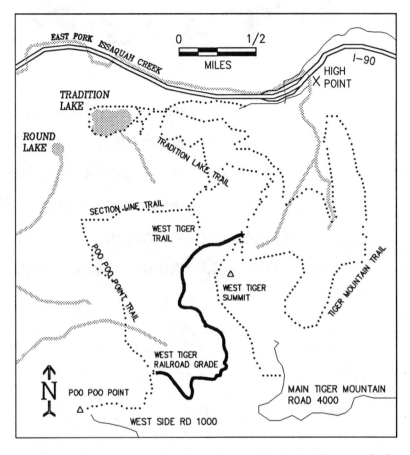

Trail, Tiger Mountain Trail, and Tradition Lake Trail. If you are look-ing for a less strenuous approach, take SR 18 to Tiger Mountain sum-mit and turn onto DNR's West Side Road 1000 to its end at Poo Poo Point. Proceed downhill on the closed portion of this road and look carefully for the West Side Railroad Grade Trail to the right.

Although this area was completely logged up until 1929, it is still a wonderful forest. The huge stumps of the original trees are still visible with springboard cuts in their sides. Many of the trees that have grown since the logging era are now sizable deciduous trees. This means that they carpet the woods and trail with multicolored leaves in the fall and allow for great views to the northwest in the winter. In the summer they provide welcome shade on hot days. Their canopy of green pre-vents significant brush from growing, allowing visitors to see consider-able distances within the forest. They also help keep moisture from evaporating, so you will find moss in many places.

Eastern

Washington

30. Ben Burr Trail
CITY OF SPOKANE PARKS

Endpoints : Liberty Park to Underhill Park
Length : 1.1 miles
Surface : unimproved dirt/lava
Restrictions : none
Original Railroad : Spokane and Inland Empire Electric Railroad, built
1905–1908, abandoned 1952–1970s, trail opened 1988
Location : Spokane, Spokane County

This rail-trail is located in the southeast part of Spokane and connects two popular city parks with good access at both ends. It is an ideal place for a quiet walk or for jogging. Because the trail is elevated above neighboring houses, there are good views of Spokane and Mount Spokane to the north.

The Spokane and Inland Empire Electric Railroad was originally built to move passengers and freight in the fast-growing Palouse farmland. It extended south to Colfax and Moscow, Idaho, and east to Coeur d'Alene. Passenger service ended on March 31, 1939, and the last freight service ended in October 1941. Portions of the line were abandoned in 1952, with the last sections of line removed in the late 1970s. The trail is named after Ben Burr, a former chief civil engineer for the Great Northern Railroad.

The former main electric generating plant for the railroad is now an apartment building.

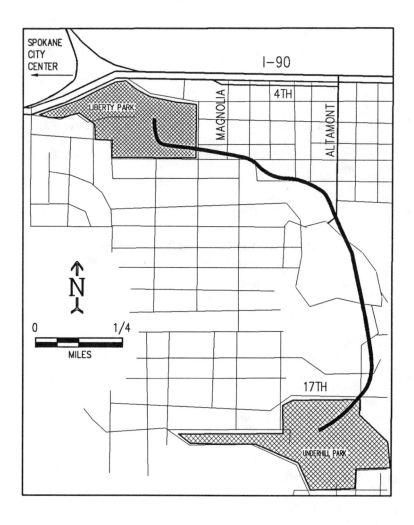

To get to the west end, take I-90 to Spokane and turn off on exit 283A (Altamont). Turn right on Altamont and right one block on Fourth Street. Follow Fourth back to the west and turn left into Liberty Park at the park sign facing the freeway. The rail-trail begins at the south end of the parking area.

The trail is primarily still in its rustic state from years of neglect. There have been few improvements along the route except for a bridge over Altamont and a concrete ramp up from Liberty Park. The remainder of the trail is in a rough, natural state with a rocky surface and brush growing alongside. This preserves its ambience as an old natural corridor in the midst of an urban area.

The trail connects two community parks, Liberty and Underhill. These parks have parking, restrooms, and ball fields. At the west end of the trail is a large brick building high on the hill. This was the main power-generating facility for the electric line and has been converted into apartments.

The rail-trail is a community development project of the South Central Community. Sometime in the future it may connect with the old railroad route going south from South Hill, near Glenrose, to Colfax, as well as connecting to the north with the Spokane River Centennial Trail.

31. Cowiche Canyon Trail
COWICHE CANYON CONSERVANCY

Endpoints : Weikel Road to Cowiche Canyon County Road
Length : 3.0 miles
Surface : natural dirt/gravel
Restrictions : no hunting, no firearms
Original Railroad : North Yakima and Valley Railroad
Location : 11 miles west of Yakima, Yakima County

A unique oasis in the dry sagebrush of eastern Washington, Cowiche Canyon is a beautiful, pristine canyon. The rail-trail follows an abandoned railroad grade through a narrow canyon cut into the rock by Cowiche Creek and provides visitors a quiet place of rock, wildlife, and vegetation.

To get to the trailhead, take I-82 to exit 33 (Yakima) and turn west onto E Yakima Avenue. Go 1.8 miles west and turn right on Summit-

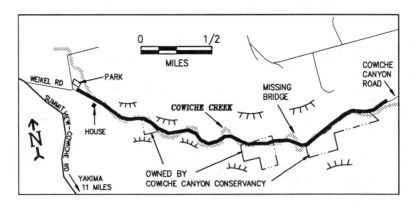

One of the many trestles over Cowiche Creek

view. Go 9.7 miles and turn right on Weikel Road. Go 0.4 mile to the Cowiche Canyon Trail sign on the right. Turn right and park in the large, open, gravel area.

This trail is ideal for walking. There is a quiet peacefulness in the narrow canyon with the creek underfoot and wildlife everywhere. While the trail can be used by bicyclists, it is not a long ride and probably will remain a dead end for several years to come.

The trail starts at the east end of the canyon with a large wooden sign describing the canyon and illustrating the trail and creek. It winds down the canyon crossing and recrossing the creek for 1.7 miles to a missing bridge. Although the creek is not very wide, even in late summer there is still considerable water—enough that you will get wet wading across it. The trail continues another 1.3 miles before ending at private property.

The canyon is a haven for naturalists, with numerous birds and small animals thriving in the grasses nurtured by the flowing creek. The area is free from any development and is close to a natural state.

The green swath along the creek is in strong contrast to the neighboring sagebrush and rock.

The north and south walls of the canyon differ considerably since the south wall is thirteen million years older than the north wall. Fourteen million years ago, lava flowed from fissures near Pullman to form the flora and south wall. One million years ago, Tieton andesite from the Goat Rocks Range created the north wall. As the trail runs back and forth across the creek, it cuts through parts of the south and north walls close enough for the visitor to see the differences in rock type.

This trail is owned and operated by the Cowiche Canyon Conservancy, a private nonprofit group that is preserving a unique ecosystem with public access. One of the main goals of the Conservancy is to preserve the land in as much of its natural state as possible.

32. Douglas Creek Trail
BUREAU OF LAND MANAGEMENT

Endpoints : Palisades to Alstown
Length : 10.0 miles
Surface : original ballast/sand/rock
Restrictions : none
Location : 3 miles southeast of Waterville, Douglas County

This rail-trail is located in a little-known part of the state with a unique natural beauty. The trail connects the low, dry sagebrush of Moses Coulee with the high plateau farmlands near Waterville. If you are tired of crowded trails, this is a place to find solitude.

The land just east of the Columbia River is normally very arid, especially at lower elevations. The existence of water makes a significant difference on the vegetation and wildlife. Badger Mountain to the west of Douglas Creek helps feed a continuous water supply to Douglas Creek, even in the heat of the summer. McCue Spring near the south end of the trail provides additional water supply year-round.

To get to the south end of the trail, take SR 26 south of Wenatchee 15 miles to Palisades Road. Go east 12 miles up Moses Coulee past Palisades to where the road turns sharply to the right. Take the first good gravel road left (north) up the hill to the left of Douglas Creek Canyon. Proceed into the canyon before parking. To get to the north end of the trail, take SR 2 to Waterville, go 1 mile east, and take Road K SW southeast 3 miles to Alstown, where there is a silver-colored grain terminal.

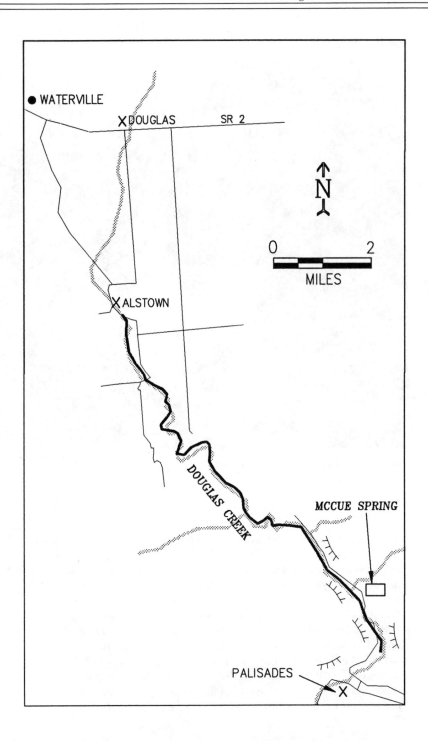

The remains of a trestle over Douglas Creek

This is a newly acquired rail-trail and development has only just begun. The condition of the trail reflects the harshness of the surroundings. The surface varies from large rocks to sand. There are numerous gravel berms created where the original culverts were removed. The missing trestles require fording of the sizable creek, although in the summer the cool water is a delight. The trail is difficult for mountain biking; hiking and horseback riding are much more appropriate.

Before you visit this rail-trail, contact the Bureau of Land Management in Wenatchee to learn the latest conditions. Also, be prepared for a very rustic hike in a remote area. Pack plenty of water and provisions and be especially careful of rattlesnakes—they love the rocky canyon walls. One of the greatest assets of this location is also one of its greatest dangers: You are not likely to see anyone along the trail.

33. Iron Horse State Park
WASHINGTON STATE PARKS
AND RECREATION COMMISSION

Endpoints : Hyak to Columbia River
Length : 88.0 miles
Surface : gravel/unimproved ballast
Restrictions : no camping, no hunting
Original Railroad : Chicago, Milwaukee, St. Paul, and Pacific Railroad
Location : Hyak, Kittitas, Kittitas County

This is a beautiful rail-trail traveling from the Cascade Mountains to the Columbia River. It offers such recreational opportunities as horse-drawn sleighs, dog-sled races, and cross-country skiing in the winter, and hiking, mountain biking, horseback riding, and wagon-pulling in the summer.

To get to the western end, take I-90 to exit 54 (Hyak). Take the first left along the frontage road and then the first right on Forest Service Road 22191 for 0.25 mile. The trailhead is on your right. To get to the eastern end take I-90 to exit 136 (Vantage) and head south 6 miles on Wanapum Road to where it crosses the rail-trail. There are several additional access points from I-90: Stampede Pass Road exit 62, Easton exit 71, West Nelson Siding Road exit 74, East Nelson Siding Road exit 78, South Cle Elum exit 84, Thorp exit 93, Ellensburg exit 106, and Kittitas exit 115.

Starting from Hyak, the trail skirts Lake Keechelus with wonderful views of the mountains. It passes through two snowsheds, which can provide shelter from various forms of precipitation that occur in the area. The portion of the right-of-way from Cabin Creek east to Easton is not yet in State Parks ownership, and the bridge is missing over the Yakima River, which you cannot wade across. Cabin Creek Road does go around this gap back up in the hills to the south and comes out at Easton.

Lake Easton State Park is the headquarters for the park rangers in charge of Iron Horse State Park. Overnight camping and water are available in the park. There is a trailhead in Easton just southeast of the frontage road. There are also mountain bike rentals and horse-drawn wagon and sleigh rides available.

The route from Easton to South Cle Elum runs parallel to I-90 but is usually out of sight to the west. South Cle Elum was a major town built around the Milwaukee Railroad operations. Here you can find a bed-and-breakfast establishment built in the old railroad crew quarters. There is a trailhead facility here next to the old railway station and a large brick building that was the power-generating facility for generating the electricity to run the engines. Electricity was preferred as a

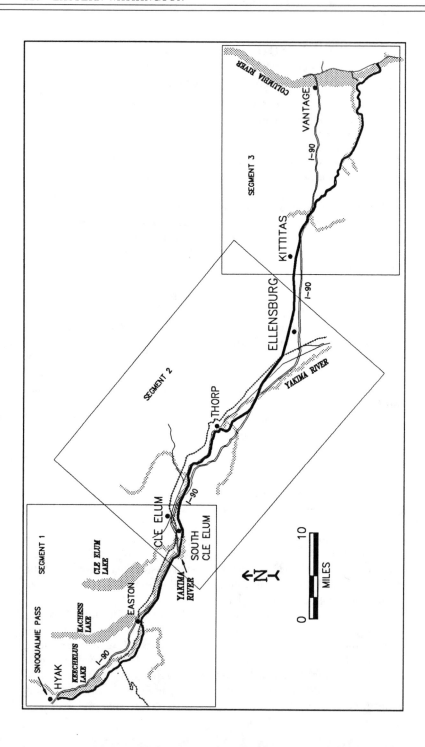

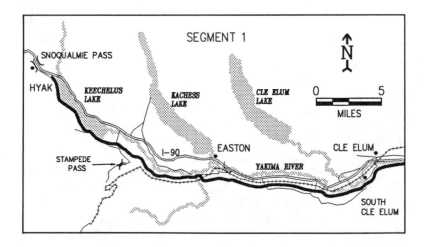

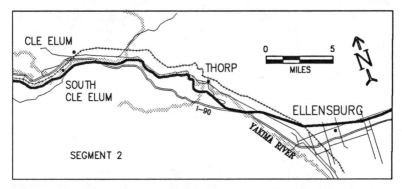

power source over coal- or steam-fired engines in the mountains, where there were long tunnels, because the smoke tended to suffocate the crews.

From South Cle Elum the trail follows the Yakima River through a narrow canyon, winding along the tight corners and through several tunnels. This is a quiet area with pine trees. You'll see an active Washington Central Railroad track on the north side of the river, and the old highway above the canyon. The trail passes through the small town of Thorp, which can be reached via exit 93 from I-90. State Parks has plans for developing a trailhead nearby. Until the trestle east is decked, you must leave the trail where it intersects SR 97. Go west on Thorp Highway across the Yakima to where it intersects Highway 10. Turn right (east) to the intersection with SR 97 to Wenatchee. Go north on SR 97 about three blocks and regain the grade going east.

Continuing east, the trail passes through Ellensburg, where Iron Horse State Park is interrupted by the Central Washington University campus. You must go north around the fencing on the east side of the campus. You can trace the route of the old railroad by following the overhead power lines.

Kittitas is the easternmost community along the rail-trail. It is a very small community with the old train station preserved as a museum, public meeting place, and park area. This is the last chance for water until Wanapum Recreation Area on the Columbia River.

The railroad crosses I-90 on a large trestle that is temporarily blocked. To cross the freeway, 2 miles east of Kittitas take the freeway crossing just south of the grade and turn left (east) on the frontage road on the south side of the freeway. Pass under the trestle and take the first road to the right, Boylston Road, which leads back up to the grade. You can find the grade by looking for the power lines.

The trail gradually climbs up to Boylston Tunnel (2,250 feet elevation), the site of a former railroad community. The tunnel is 1,973 feet long, with a slight curve at the west end. Be prepared with a flashlight and watch for horned owls in the rock cuts at both ends of the tunnel. Just east of the tunnel is a watering place for livestock and a meadow.

From here to the Columbia River—about 18 miles—the trail is all downhill at a 2.2 percent grade. About 16 miles from Kittitas is an old homestead and corrals, a part of the Old West that hasn't changed over

Wagons descend the grade near the Columbia River.

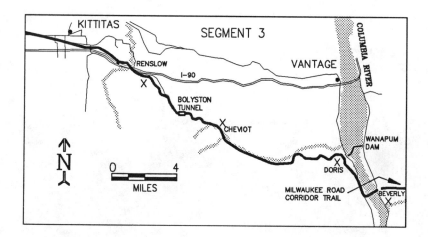

the last hundred years. The grade lies in the drainage of Johnson Creek and descends to the Columbia River at an elevation of 580 feet.

Crossing the Columbia River is a long, steel bridge. This bridge has railway ties, but no decking, and is closed to public use. There are no services or facilities at the bridge, but the Washington State Parks and Recreation Commission operates the Wanapum Recreation Area 3 miles north along a country road, and there are services 6 miles north at Vantage. Note how the Columbia River has cut through the Saddle Mountains to the south.

This is very dry country, and all users should be prepared with adequate water and food. There are no services of any kind on the trail itself and generally no public roads nearby. Also be forewarned that the army practices maneuvers just over the ridge to the south, and you may hear occasional booming. The army would like to take over the trail from Boylston to the Columbia River and the land all the way north to the freeway to expand its Yakima Firing Range.

This trail is very popular in the winter for cross-country skiing and other snow sports. For example, the Snow King Alaskan Malamute Fanciers hold their annual Freight Race on the trail in South Cle Elum each January. Horse-drawn sleigh rides are offered from Hyak when there is sufficient snow. Most of the route is generally safe from avalanches (stay in the snowsheds!), and its level terrain makes it ideal for beginning cross-country skiers.

This trail was opened in 1984 from Easton 25 miles east to tunnel 47. This portion of the trail was named the John Wayne Pioneer Trail at the behest of the citizens' group that helped convince the legislature to acquire the entire right-of-way in 1981. In 1989 State Parks' ownership was extended to the Columbia River and in the future may include the remainder of the Milwaukee Road Corridor all the way to Idaho.

This sign says it all.

34. Lower Yakima Pathway
CITY OF GRANDVIEW PARKS AND RECREATION,
CITY OF SUNNYSIDE PARKS AND RECREATION,
YAKIMA COUNTY PARKS AND RECREATION

Endpoints : Grandview to Sunnyside
Length : 6.3 miles
Surface : asphalt
Restrictions : none
Original Railroad : active Washington Central Railroad
Location : Grandview, Sunnyside, Yakima County

This trail is located on a railroad right-of-way next to a busy road. It provides a safe place for walking and bicycling and connects two small communities. It exemplifies how an active railroad right-of-way can serve a compatible use.

To get to the north trailhead in Sunnyside, follow I-82 to Sunnyside and take exit 67. Turn right onto Yakima Valley Highway and proceed to 16th Street. There is a park-and-ride lot at the start of the trail, which runs southeast between the highway and the railroad. To reach the south trailhead in Grandview, take exit 73 (Stover Road) to Grandview and turn southeast toward town. You'll find a park-and-ride lot just south of Stover Road, where the rail-trail starts and heads north.

Lower Valley County Park is located about 2 miles south of the Sunnyside trailhead. It has restroom facilities, water, and shade, all useful in this area. Nearby there is a wine-tasting room for one of the many wineries in the Yakima Valley.

This rail-trail is an example of an innovative project initiated by local citizens, who contributed much volunteer labor, and involving the cooperation of several agencies. The project was started by the General Federation of Women's Clubs of Lower Yakima Valley, and the trail is

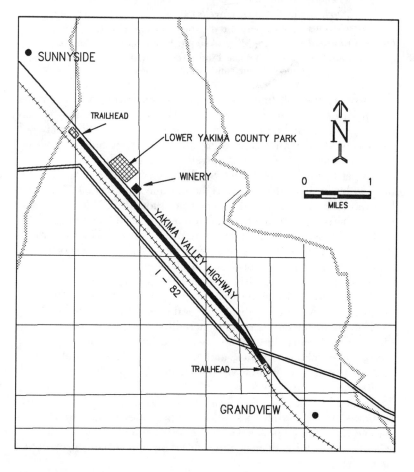

co-managed by the cities of Sunnyside and Grandview and Yakima County Parks. The land has been protected from development because of the railroad and highway easements. It now serves a useful purpose by providing a nonmotorized route between two local communities along a very busy highway.

35. Milwaukee Road Corridor Trail
DEPARTMENT OF NATURAL RESOURCES

Endpoints : Idaho border to Columbia River
Length : 180.0 miles
Surface : loose ballast/gravel/sand
Restrictions : use by permit only; some portions closed
Original Railroad : Chicago, Milwaukee, St. Paul, and Pacific Railroad
Location : Tekoa, Rosalia, Lind, Warden, Othello, Beverly in Whitman, Adams, and Grant counties

To travel this rail-trail is an adventure, one where you can relive the experiences of the early pioneers. The land and the rail-trail are rugged, with many hidden treasures along the way. Unlike many rail-trails in western Washington, there are always tremendous views because there are no large stands of trees lining the route.

To get to the east end, take SR 27 to Tekoa and look for the high railroad bridge over town. Turn right on Lone Pine Road 0.25 mile before the railroad bridge and proceed up a long hill. Where the road takes a sharp right, turn left on a dirt road and go 100 feet to get to the trail. Access is also good at the only other "towns" along the route: Rosalia, Lind, and Warden. The west access is at Beverly, 6 miles south of the I-90 Vantage Bridge on SR 243.

Because of the long distances between access points, this trail is most appropriate for equestrian or mountain bike use. However, people have walked the entire route and enjoyed it considerably.

The wildlife along the route is incredible. Be prepared to see many different birds, including hawks, owls, and terns. Also look for porcupines, deer, rabbits, coyotes, and rattlesnakes. The right-of-way has preserved a strip of natural vegetation that is often the only wildlife habitat for miles around.

Remember that this is wild land with wild animals. The author was reminded of this while passing through a rock cut: A rattlesnake warned him, and he pedaled faster. Another time a coyote reappeared several times atop a distant bluff, observing the author's progress for several miles.

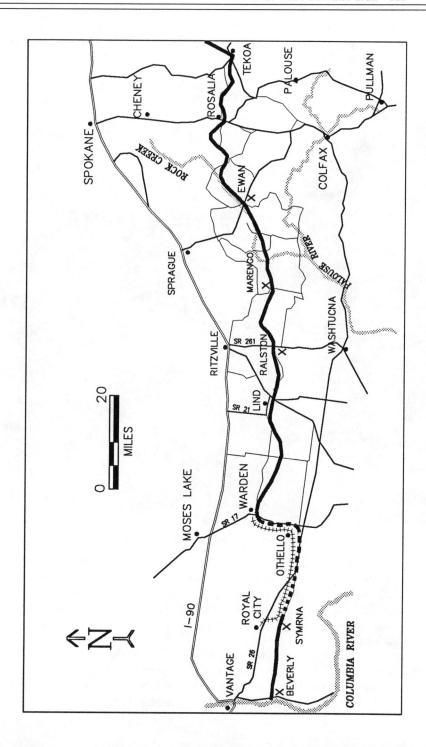

The spectacular route along the basalt cliffs of Rock Lake

Grain elevators were originally built along the route because the railroad was the only way to get grain to markets. Now the grain elevators are the lighthouses in this dry sea; they mark old train stations, road intersections, and sometimes small communities. They become welcome sights to the weary traveler.

The trail begins at 2,686 feet in the Palouse Hills at the Idaho border and ends at 545 feet on the Columbia River, passing through four different geographic areas. Starting in the pine forest foothills of the Rocky Mountains, it passes through the Palouse Hills and the dry scablands around Rock Lake, across the barren Rattlesnake Plateau, and down the Lind Coulee to Crab Creek and to the mighty Columbia River. The natural terrain changes throughout the trip. Pine trees in the eastern Palouse give way to rolling hills with no trees for miles until Malden, where there are pine trees at a lower elevation. From Malden the trail runs alongside Pine Creek, with lush marshes and green vegetation all the way to Rock Lake. Rock Lake has steep basalt cliffs and pine trees its entire length. Below Rock Lake the trail climbs gradually to a high plateau of scablands, scrub grass, and basalt cliffs. At Ralston the trail enters the Lind Coulee with a dry creekbed and grasslands. The last section, from Othello to the Columbia, lies in a broad valley between two hillsides where there are sand dunes and small lakes.

Travel on this trail is serious business. There are very few sources of food or water along the entire route and significant distances between supplies. Be prepared to undo barbed-wire gates and replace them after passing through. The Department of Natural Resources (DNR) has not developed the trail surface at all; it varies from hard-packed gravel to soft gravel to uneven large gravel that is hard on feet, hooves, and bike tires.

The towns along this route range from very small to unrecognizable. The only available food is at Tekoa, Rosalia, Lind, Warden, and Othello. There is drinking water available at the gas station in Malden and at the town park in Ralston. Other names on the accompanying map are of old railway stations that used to dot this route and were created to provide water stops for the big steam locomotives. Too bad they don't still exist to quench the thirst of the trail traveler.

The trail is used every year by the John Wayne Pioneer Wagons and Riders group, which sponsors a wagon train. During the 1989 Washington State Centennial celebration more than 500 people participated in a wagon train crossing Washington State on this trail.

This rail-trail is so long that the most useful way to describe it is by geographic zones.

Palouse

Idaho Border to Rosalia, 26 miles

The trail unofficially starts at Tekoa near the Idaho border. (The trail actually begins at the Idaho border 5.6 miles east of Tekoa, where it is accessible by a few county roads.) Tekoa is a small town with one cafe and one grocery. The Milwaukee Road, the common name for the Chicago, Milwaukee, St. Paul, and Pacific Railroad, was designed to go across the top hills of the Palouse while the other railroads ran in the valley bottoms. Consequently, when the Milwaukee Road Corridor Trail passes through Tekoa, it is on a huge trestle over Slippery Gulch. The trestle is so prominent that it is used as the background for the

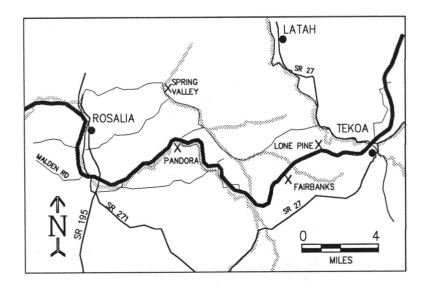

town's business cards. The trestle is currently closed; so to get to the trail going west, go north on Highway 27 out of town and turn left at the first bridge over the creek onto Lone Pine Road. Climb to the top of the hill and take a left 100 feet on a farmer's dirt road to the rail-trail. The trestle's west approach is 1.3 miles east from this point.

The trail paints a swath of green across the Palouse Hills. These hills were formed by years of prevailing easterly winds blowing topsoil to this location, and they are now quite productive. The 100-foot right-of-way has not been farmed, but every other inch of land has. This makes the trail a ribbon of green draped across the tops of the hills. The trail gradually drops in elevation alongside the hills and crosses into Rosalia on a beautiful concrete arch bridge. Rosalia is a little town with a grocery and a wonderful park. Take the first paved road crossing to reach the center of town.

Pines
Rosalia to Ewan, 29 miles

The trail through Rosalia lies on a hillside and is not easily accessible. To regain the grade, go out of town to the north and take the first road (Gashous Road) that crosses the creek to your left. Take the first dirt road to the right that climbs up to the right-of-way. Traveling north out of Rosalia, you will soon see the large, beautiful Rosalia cemetery on your left. Pine trees line the trail as it follows Pine Creek west. The bridge over Pine Creek provides a beautiful view of a lowland field to the south rimmed with pine trees.

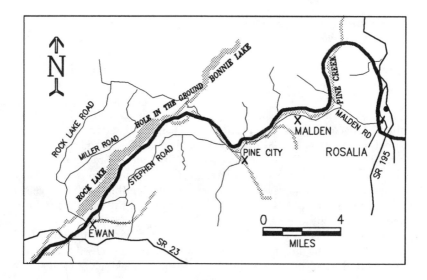

Malden is the next town. It used to be a main railroad town with many railroad maintenance facilities. Today it is a very quiet, small community with one gas station that has drinking water. The old railway station is still in place, although it has seen much better days.

The route from here to Ewan has one gap of private ownership necessitating a detour around all of Rock Lake. You can proceed on either side of the lake on local dirt roads, but unfortunately they do not offer much of a view of the lake. Leave the grade either at Stephen Road to go around the east side or Miller Road for the west side. It is possible to go part way down the lake on the trail before you need to backtrack, and it is well worth it. This is one of the most picturesque parts of the entire trail.

If you continue on to Rock Lake you will pass over a large steel-girder bridge on a curve over Pine Creek. There are still two steel boxcars lying on their sides where they fell off the trestle just before the line was abandoned. Just around the curve is a view of the area known as Hole in the Ground, a narrow canyon about 300 feet below.

Rock Lake is a 7-mile-long lake with steep basalt cliffs on all sides. The railroad was carved along the edge of the lake about 300 feet above the water. You will pass through several tunnels and over some very "airy" trestles, which make the view even more spectacular. When you come to a wheat combine buried in the dirt across the trail, you have reached the private property. At the southern end of Rock Lake the right-of-way is still 100 feet above the lake level and provides a spectacular view up the lake to the north.

Scablands
Ewan to Warden, 72 miles

Ewan is a community with a few houses and a grain elevator and no public services. The right-of-way is private for 0.4 mile north and 0.7 mile south of town. Going south you'll find a parallel county road. Take the first left onto a small gravel road to regain the grade.

This area is called scablands as it is trying to heal itself from the tremendous scouring that occurred when at least 30 separate ice dams broke in Montana 12,000 to 14,000 years ago and released incredible amounts of water. These are known as the Spokane or Bretz floods, and they flowed over lower eastern Washington from here to the present course of the Columbia River to the west. During the floods this land was under 800 feet of water and was scoured by all the rock debris, removing most of the soils.

This land has no trees of any kind. It is so rocky that it cannot be farmed except in the creek bottoms. But you'll find real wildness and beauty in the shapes carved into the rocks and in looking out to the horizon and not seeing human intervention in the land (except for the railway grade). The land is used as range land for cattle, but because it is so marginal there are few cattle per acre. There may be more deer than cows. It is the home of many wild animals: deer, coyotes, horned owls in every rock cut, jack rabbits, hawks, mice, grasshoppers, and birds.

Going west from Ewan you will come to a small area known as Revere, where the trail crosses Revere Road. The land near the grain terminal is still private land, so just use the county road alongside until 0.2 mile west of the grain terminal.

The dramatic nature of the scablands is exemplified at Cow Creek. The railroad built a huge steel trestle across this creek. It has been removed, thus creating a bit of a workout for trail users. The view to the valley floor 200 feet below is wonderful. There you will see contented cows grazing on the only green grass for miles. It is so quiet you can hear every one of them moan. This is rattlesnake country, so be careful, especially in rock cuts.

Unfortunately, although the DNR owns a 200-foot right-of-way across the valley floor, there is no safe way to get to it because of the rock cliffs. That's why the railroad built a trestle here. To bypass the missing Cow Creek trestle, at Marengo take the county road on the south side of the trail and take the first right northwest into Cow Creek. Take the next sharp left and then the next right, climbing out of the valley and up and across the grade in about 1 mile.

The town of Ralston has three houses, no services, and a little park with a public drinking faucet. The trail from here to Lind parallels the

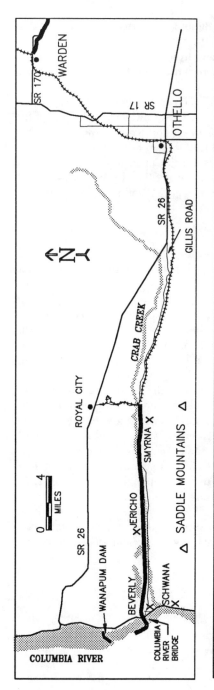

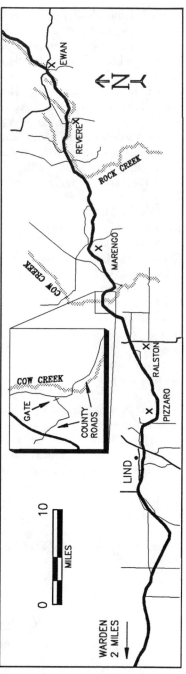

Lind–Ralston Road through continuous sagebrush and land that is gentler than that you have passed through.

Lind is a town with services, laundromat, motel, cafe, and grocery. There used to be a large trestle across the Lind Coulee but it was removed for the steel.

The next section is a long 24 miles down a very dry, flat, sagebrush valley away from any roads. Again the trail is away from the rest of the world. It is easy to imagine why pioneers kept going west.

At Warden the trail ends, and the next 36 miles are an active railroad. The best alternative route is via the main highway to Othello. From Othello go west 8 miles on highway 26 and turn left (south) on Gillis Road (gravel) and you will intersect the trail in 23 miles.

Creek Marshes
Smyrna to Beverly, 16 miles

Now the trail is at a lower elevation (600 feet) and follows Crab Creek to the Columbia River. Much of the land to the north of the trail is federal or state wildlife habitat.

The station stops of Smyrna and Jericho were named for places in the Bible. There are still homes at Smyrna, and if you look carefully you will see the old schoolhouse. The only remnant of the former station at Jericho is a log building that is still standing. Just several hundred feet north of the trail are three lakes that have excellent fishing and many fishing enthusiasts.

Beverly is a small community next to the Columbia, but the only public service is a post office. The old Beverly railway station is still standing in good repair. The Columbia River Bridge is closed to public access, but it is amazing to see. Going west, the trail connects with Iron Horse State Park at the west side of the Columbia River Bridge.

This trail is operated by the DNR, and permits must be obtained only from trail manager James Munroe; telephone (509) 925-6131. Be sure to ask for a key for the numerous gates.

This rail-trail comprises a significant portion of the Washington Cross-State Trail and needs citizen support to get it developed for easy and safe passage. It has the potential for being an important part of the Washington Cross-State Trail.

36. Neppel Landing Trail
MOSES LAKE PARKS AND RECREATION

Endpoints : Alder Street to trail end
Length : 0.5 mile
Surface : concrete
Restrictions : no horses
Original Railroad : active Washington Central Railway
Location : Moses Lake, Grant County

This is a great place to stroll along the water near the downtown area of Moses Lake. The concrete surface winds back and forth across the existing railroad track and is surrounded by green grass. A small pier offers access to a good view of the lake.

To get to the trailhead, from I-90 take exit 179 north on Highway 17 (Broadway) to downtown Moses Lake. Turn left (west) on Alder Street and Neppel Landing Park will be on your left. There is parking between the park and the buildings on Broadway.

A metal-sculpture wild horse terrorizes the park.

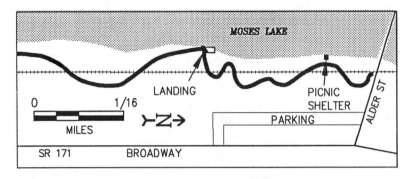

The current trail is the beginning of a longer rail-trail along the water in downtown Moses Lake. It was created by a local downtown civic organization and is operated by the city parks department. If abandonment of the railroad line occurs in the future, the trail could be extended in both directions for a total length of more than 2 miles.

37. Pacific Crest Scenic Trail
U.S. FOREST SERVICE, SKYKOMISH RANGER STATION

> *Endpoints* : Stevens Pass to Yodelin
> *Length* : 1.5 miles
> *Surface* : dirt
> *Restrictions* : no bicycles, winter travel *not recommended*
> *Original Railroad* : Great Northern Railway, built 1892, abandoned 1900
> *Location* : Stevens Pass, Chelan County

The Pacific Scenic Crest Trail by necessity has to pass across Highway 2 at Stevens Pass. Instead of climbing the steep ridge to the north of the pass, it follows the original railroad grade built in 1892 that went over Stevens Pass before the first tunnel was built in 1900.

This trail is a great place to take an easy walk in the high mountains. It's also a good place to get out and stretch your legs while driving through Stevens Pass.

To get to the trailhead, take Highway 2 to Stevens Pass. Turn off at the parking lot to the north and go behind the green-roofed, A-frame building at the back and east of the parking area.

The trail is the original Great Northern Railway route over Stevens Pass. This high route was abandoned when the first tunnel was constructed in 1900. A second tunnel was constructed in 1929, creating a

A lone hiker enjoys the Pacific Crest Trail.

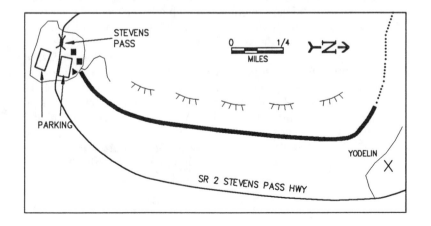

third route. The second route through the first tunnel will be converted to a rail-trail opening in 1993.

The Pacific Scenic Crest Trail continues on from where it leaves the railroad grade up to Lake Valhalla. It enters the Henry M. Jackson Wilderness at 2 miles from Stevens Pass. Look for the Stevens Pass Historic District signs and the Iron Goat Trail, scheduled to open in 1993.

Caution: Do NOT use this route in the winter as it is extremely prone to avalanches.

38. Republic Rail-Trail
REPUBLIC PARKS DISTRICT

Endpoints : high school to fairgrounds
Length : 3.2 miles
Surface : gravel/sand
Restrictions : none; motorized vehicles permitted
Original Railroad : Washington and Great Northern Railroad, built 1902
Location : Republic to Sanpoil, Ferry County

This rail-trail is a local trail through the lower part of Republic out to the county fairgrounds east of town. It provides a good route connecting the city, high school, and fairgrounds. It also provides a safe alternative route to SR 21, a fairly busy highway.

Republic is a city developed around the major mining claims in the area, some of which are still active and productive. There were numerous railroad lines going to the mines and up into the woods for logging. This line was the main line running north toward Curlew, where it connected with the Northern Pacific line.

To get to the west end of the trail, go to downtown Republic, turn west on Ninth Street, and go one block to Ripple Ball Field. The trail begins to the southeast below the steep bank below the main street. To get to the east end, go to the fairgrounds 3 miles east of town and look north across the highway for a public trail access to the rail-trail 400 feet north of the highway.

The rail-trail is built into the hillside above a marshy area that provides good wildlife viewing. It generally remains some distance from the main highway and goes through several deep cuts in the rock.

The end of the railroad line

This rail-trail is open to motorized vehicles because they are very popular in this community. The route had been used by ORV's for years before the Parks District's purchase, and there is an established use to bypass the state highway.

In the future, if the railroad line north is abandoned, there is the potential for this rail-trail to continue to Curlew and perhaps to Canada. The road west from Curlew, West Kettle River Road, is located on the original Northern Pacific Railroad right-of-way.

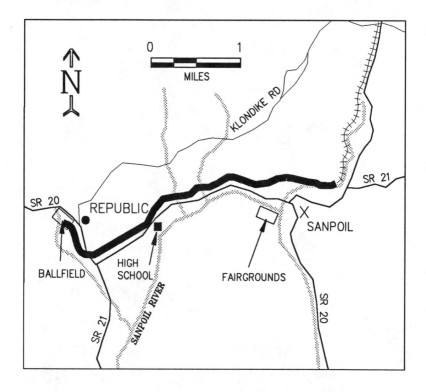

39. Scablands Nature Corridor
WASHINGTON STATE PARKS
AND RECREATION COMMISSION

Endpoints : Fish Lake to East Pasco
Length : 132.0 miles
Surface : large, rough ballast
Restrictions : none
Original Railroad : Spokane, Portland, and Seattle Railroad, built 1908, abandoned 1991
Location . Cheney, Spokane County, to Pasco, Franklin County

This railroad corridor has several special attributes. The right-of-way on both sides of the grade itself is a natural area, and the corridor is surrounded by land that is almost completely undeveloped. There is extensive railroad history, part of which is preserved in the railroad grade itself. The route was one of the state's early transportation corridors. It also follows the path of a major geological event that had a significant impact on all of eastern Washington.

Between 12,000 and 14,000 years ago a series of tremendous floods caused by broken ice dams in Montana roared through most of southeastern Washington. The Bretz Floods, named after the geologist who identified their existence, released huge amounts of water that covered Spokane more than 800 feet deep. The tremendous volume of water flowed south down to the Columbia River, scouring gullies in the solid basalt rock from the Palouse Hills west to the Cascades. The resulting land has been called the scablands because the land is still trying to heal itself from these tremendous events. The rail-trail follows the path of the flood waters, whose work is still visible along the entire route.

This line was built by the Spokane, Portland, and Seattle Railroad. While it was not the first line connecting Spokane southwest to Portland, it was designed to be the best, with the easiest grades and gentlest curves. Much of the railroad right-of-way follows the route of the Mullen Trail. This 644-mile wagon route was established in 1868 but abandoned in 1872, when railroads began to provide faster transportation. There are several markers of this route along the corridor. A stone monument in Lamont was erected in 1925 by the Washington Historical Society showing where the Mullen Trail passed.

The dry weather is kind to old artifacts. You can still see old buildings that were built at the turn of the century. The grain elevators built along the railroad are also testimony to the importance of the railroad to the area's growth. The old water tower at Benge is still in good condition and is used as the town's water storage facility.

This corridor is generally undeveloped, except for some grazing areas and a few farms. It provides a wonderful opportunity for viewing wildlife. There are numerous rock depressions, caused by the great floods, that hold water year-round, providing invaluable habitat for wildlife in an otherwise very dry part of the state.

At its north end, the trail passes through Turnbull National Wildlife Refuge, created specifically to provide habitat for the breeding of birds. Ducks Unlimited also owns some property adjacent to the corridor that is being preserved for the same purpose. The trail user has an opportunity to view these areas since the corridor often passes close to ponds, lakes, and creeks. This is only "natural" as the railroad's engineers always sought out waterways, which are naturally gradual paths through rocky landscapes. Some of the landowners adjacent to the corridor have also set aside their lands as wildlife preserves.

The construction of the railroad itself has actually created wildlife habitat. In many places the gravel grade has created small ponds that have become nesting sites for birds. There are numerous cuts in the rock along this route that have become natural home sites for owls, rattlesnakes, and other animals. The lower part of the corridor alongside the Snake River passes through ideal habitat for large raptors. The four steel trestles provide airy nesting sites for swallows.

To get to the north end of the trail, take I-90 to Cheney. Go 3 miles northeast on Spokane–Cheney Road to Myers Park Road at the north end of Fish Lake. To get to the south end, take SR 12 through Pasco to Pasco–Kahlotus Road and proceed east 4.8 miles. Turn right (south) on Martindale Road, signed "Dead End" and "Primitive Road." Go 1.4 miles and angle left on Mehlenbacker Farm Road for 0.8 mile to the grade. There is good access to the Snake River here. Sacajawea State Park is across SR 12 in the opposite direction at the confluence of the Columbia and Snake rivers. Other good access points are 0.5 mile east from Cheney on Cheney Plaza Road, at Amber, at Downs Lake 8 miles east of Sprague, and at Lamont, Benge, Washtucna, and Kahlotus.

The corridor starts at Fish Lake, one of the numerous lakes in this region carved out of basalt by the Bretz Floods. The elevation is sufficient to capture moisture to support scattered pine trees and lush grasses. But the topsoil is very thin, and rock cliffs and outcrops are visible everywhere.

About 4 miles south of Fish Lake the corridor passes within 1 mile of Cheney, the largest community along the entire route. The grade passes beneath Cheney–Spangle Road, which leads directly into downtown Cheney. There are two old train stations there, one of which is now a restaurant.

Going south from Cheney, the corridor passes through Turnbull National Wildlife Refuge, a haven for animal watchers. Please stay on the grade through this area and enjoy the wildlife with binoculars and long lenses.

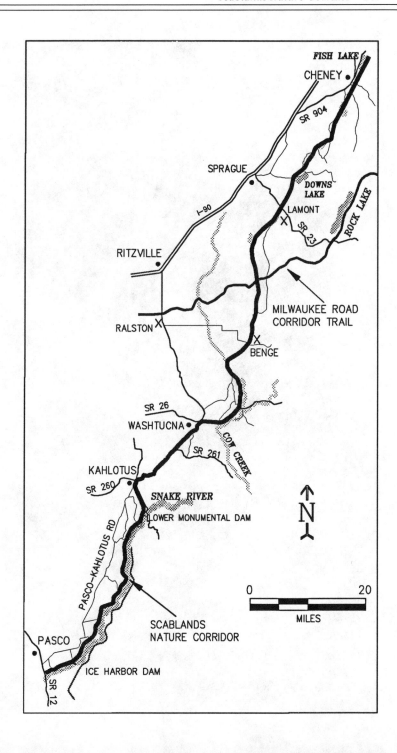

South of the refuge the trees thin out to where, at Amber, there is nothing to obstruct the view. To the east are the beginnings of the Palouse Hills and rolling wheat fields. To the south and west is a broad vista of low ridges and rocky draws. The corridor passes close to Amber Lake, which has good public access and good fishing.

Several miles south of Amber Lake the grade was built up across a wide coulee. This "fill" is more than 1 mile long, and the scars from where the fill material was gathered are still very clear around the north end. Downs Lake is close by with public access. The grade enters a region of more rugged rock cliffs and small lakes on its way to Lamont. Lamont boasts a new school, a few houses, and the common grain elevator located alongside the old railroad grade. There are no public facilities in Lamont.

South of Lamont the corridor follows several dry washes for 23 miles to Benge. This is one of the most remote stretches of the entire route, with no roads alongside or crossing it for miles. Benge is a very small town with a grocery open daily from 8:00 A.M. to 5:00 P.M. except Sundays and holidays. There is a small town park across the street from the grocery.

South of Benge the grade enters Cow Creek, which goes north to Sprague and is one of the largest drainages in the region. Between Benge and Kahlotus the canyons get larger and the cliffs steeper. Near Ankeny the grade passes across a large steel trestle and then over the Union Pacific's active line just before that line enters a tunnel, a very scenic place to watch trains. Below are the lush green pastures fed by the water from Cow Creek. Across the valley next to the road is a historical marker describing the Mullen Trail. In the valley below you can see a stone house, one of several built by early settlers who were attracted to Cow Creek because of the water it supplied.

At Hooper Junction the railroad parallels SR 26, the site of another Mullen Trail historic sign. The grade passes under the highway and across a second large steel trestle to Washtucna, named after a local Indian chief. The railroad surveyors were so intent on keeping an easy grade that it ended up partway up the ridge 0.25 mile southeast of town. Farther south the corridor is located across the valley between Washtucna and Kahlotus and skirts the south side of Lake Kahlotus. Kahlotus is an Indian name meaning "hole in the ground," which describes the feeling you have being on the valley floor of the Washtucna Coulee.

At Kahlotus the grade enters a tunnel into Devil's Canyon, a steep, narrow canyon dropping quickly to the Snake River. The railroad could

The water tower at Benge is still in use.

not match the steep gradient of the canyon and therefore was carved along the rocky hillside. Rounding the corner overlooking the Snake River through another tunnel, you will be greeted with a spectacular view of the lower Snake River Canyon. Below is the old railroad grade; the portions downstream were flooded when the Ice Harbor Dam was built. Heading downstream you will pass over four tall steel trestles over Box, Wilson, Bouvey, and Burr canyons. These steel structures were built in 1908 by the American Bridge Company and are listed on the state and federal historical registers.

As you pass along this route you will be able to hear the rumble of the trains from the south side of the Snake River and watch boats far below on the Snake. There are numerous birds living on the rocky cliffs next to the grade and in the trestle girders. There are some public facilities, including campgrounds and restrooms, at Lower Monumental Dam and Ice Harbor Dam.

The grade gradually descends closer to the Snake River by the time it reaches Pasco. The current trail ends where it crosses Mehlenbacker Farm Road. There is good access to the river via this road to the left.

Be well prepared when you travel this rail-trail. The only dependable drinking water is found at Fish Lake, Amber, Lamont, Benge, Washtucna, and Kahlotus. Washtucna has a grocery, restaurants, and a motel. Kahlotus has a restaurant. Carry food, water, maps, and a snake-bite kit. Roads crossing the corridor are few and far between. The best time to travel this corridor is from April through June and in the fall.

40. Spokane River Centennial Trail
WASHINGTON STATE PARKS
AND RECREATION COMMISSION

Endpoints : Idaho to Nine Mile Dam
Length : 39 miles
Surface : paved
Restrictions : none
Original Railroad : several
Location : Spokane, Spokane County

This trail is a wonderful example of an urban trail leading into suburban and rural areas—in this case, the Spokane area. It is also a link with the Centennial Trail in Idaho that extends from the Idaho border to Coeur d'Alene.

This trail is suitable for different uses at different locations. The

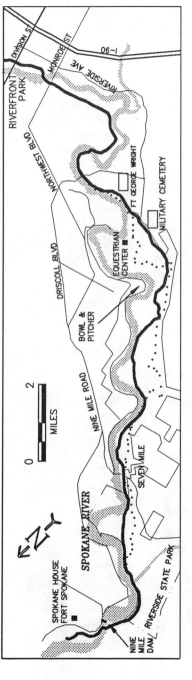

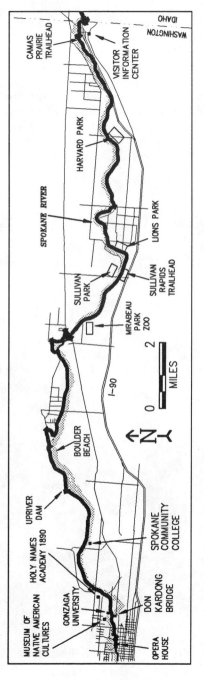

west end near downtown Spokane gets the highest volume of walkers and strollers. The paved areas to the east make terrific bike routes. Farther east in the "Valley" are less crowded areas that are more popular with equestrians.

The most popular place to use the trail is in downtown Spokane next to the Opera House. This area was redeveloped for the Spokane Expo in 1972. There is a wonderful park on an island. The trail lies next to the Spokane River and passes the convention center, large hotels, and office buildings.

Don Kardong Bridge is named after a local runner who started the

The Don Kardong Bridge, near downtown Spokane

annual Bloomsday Road Race for runners, the second largest in the United States. The bridge is an old railway bridge that has been beautifully turned into an attractive viewpoint of the Spokane River. On the north bank across the river is the Museum of Native American Cultures and Gonzaga University.

The route runs alongside an active railroad and then follows Upriver Drive for several miles until it crosses the river to the south side on a new bridge built just for the trail.

A unique attraction is a zoo located adjacent to the trail. Here the river has lower banks, and the trail is sometimes right down in the flood plain along the water's edge.

The trail crosses the Spokane River several times going east, taking advantage of the best land for a multiple-use trail. It is always close to the river and provides good access for nonmotorized boaters.

At the Idaho border the trail connects with the Idaho Centennial Trail, which continues east into downtown Coeur d'Alene.

This trail is a result of the efforts of a strong community committee specifically organized for its development. Major federal funding came through the assistance of the Honorable Thomas Foley, Speaker of the House of Representatives and a native of Spokane. In the future the trail will be developed to continue to the west of Nine Mile Dam down the Spokane River another 12 miles to Little Falls Dam.

APPENDIX 1:

Trail Managers

Bureau of Land Management
Jim Fisher, Supervisor
1133 N Western
Wenatchee, WA 98801
(509) 662-4223

City of Bellingham Parks and Recreation
Tim Wahl, Parks Planner
210 Lotti Street
Bellingham, WA 98225
(206) 676-6985

City of Grandview
Michael Carpenter, Director of Parks
207 W Second Street
Grandview, WA 98930
(509) 882-9219

City of Issaquah Parks and Recreation Department
Kerry Anderson, Director of Parks
135 E Sunset Way
Issaquah, WA 98027
(206) 391-1008

City of Kent Parks and Recreation Department
Barney Wilson, Director
220 Fourth Avenue S
Kent, WA 98032
(206) 859-3350

City of Moses Lake Parks and Recreation
Cecil Lee, Director
401 S Balsam
P.O. Box 1579
Moses Lake, WA 98837
(509) 766-9240

City of North Bend
> Pat Osborn, Public Works Director
> P.O. Box 896
> North Bend, WA 98045
> (206) 888-1211

City of Port Angeles Parks and Recreation
> Scott Brodhun, Director of Parks and Recreation
> 240 W Front
> Port Angeles, WA 98362
> (206) 457-0411, ext. 215

City of Seattle Engineering Department
> Peter Lagerwey
> 210 Municipal Building
> 600 Fourth Avenue
> Seattle, WA 98104
> (206) 684-8022

City of Snoqualmie Park Board
> Leroy Gmazel
> P.O. Box 987
> Snoqualmie, WA 98065
> (206) 888-1555

City of Spokane Parks and Recreation
> Frank McCoy, Director
> W 808 Spokane Falls Boulevard
> Spokane, WA 99201-3317
> (509) 456-2620

City of Sunnyside Parks and Recreation
> Thomas Byer, Director
> 818 E Edison Avenue
> Sunnyside, WA 98944
> (509) 837-8660

Cowiche Canyon Conservancy
> Rich Faith
> P.O. Box 877
> Yakima, WA 98907
> (509) 575-4124

Department of Natural Resources:

Milwaukee Road Corridor Trail
Jim Munroe, Milwaukee Corridor Specialist
715 E Bowers Road
Ellensburg, WA 98926
(509) 925-6131

West Tiger Mountain Railroad Grade
Preston Railroad Trail
Doug McClelland, Issaquah Unit Forester
Tiger Mountain State Forest
P. O. Box 68
Enumclaw, WA 98022
(206) 825-1631

King County Parks
Tom Eksten, King County Trails Coordinator
1612 Smith Tower
506 Second Avenue
Seattle, WA 98104
(206) 296-7800

Olympic National Park
Carl Newman
Storm King Ranger Station
HC62 Box 10
Port Angeles, WA 98362
(206) 928-3380

Republic Parks District
Larry Beardslee
County Courthouse
Republic, WA 99166
(509) 775-5231

Snohomish County Parks and Recreation
Mike Parmon
3000 Rockefeller
Everett, WA 98201
(206) 388-6621

U.S. Forest Service, Skykomish Ranger Station
P. O. Box 305
Skykomish, WA 98288
(206) 677-2414

Washington State Parks and Recreation Commission:

Franklin-Kummer Trail
>Dennis Myers, Manager
>Palmer-Kanasket State Park
>32101 Kanasket–Cumberland Road
>Palmer, WA 98051
>(206) 886-0148

Iron Horse State Park
>Colleen McKee, Park Ranger
>Lake Easton State Park
>P.O. Box 26
>Easton, WA 98925
>(509) 656-2230

Scablands Nature Corridor
>Glen Reiswig, Supervisor, Region IV Office
>2501 Sacajawea Park Road
>Pasco, WA 99301
>(509) 545-2315

Snoqualmie Pass Trail
>Doug Whisman, Area Manager
>Lake Sammamish State Park
>20606 SE 56th Street
>Issaquah, WA 98027
>(206) 455-7010

Spokane River Centennial Trail
>Gary Herron
>Riverside State Park
>4427 N Aubry Lane White Parkway
>Spokane, WA 99205
>(509) 456-3964

Sylvia Creek Trail
>Don Hansen, Park Manager
>Lake Sylvia State Park
>P.O. Box 701
>Montesano, WA 98563
>(206) 249-3621

Wallace Falls Railway Grade
>Kevin Kratochuvil, Park Ranger
>P.O. Box 106
>Gold Bar, WA 98251
>(206) 793-0420

Whatcom County Parks and Recreation
Roger DeSpain, Director of Parks and Recreation
3373 Mount Baker Highway
Bellingham, WA 98226
(206) 733-2900

Yakima County Parks and Recreation
Dan Hesse, Director
1000 Ahtanum Road
Yakima, WA 98901
(509) 575-4363

APPENDIX 2:

Future Rail-Trails

Bay to Baker Rail-Trail
Several agencies are planning a cooperative rail-trail project that would extend from Bellingham Bay to Glacier in Whatcom County.

Black Diamond Trail
This King County Parks project is in the land acquisition stage. The trail will extend from Maple Falls to Black Diamond, perhaps continuing to the Franklin Bridge over the Green River.

Cedar River Trail
This trail is a King County Parks project and will go from Renton to Landsburg County Park along the Cedar River. The railroad line was abandoned in 1991 and the right-of-way was purchased by King County. The western portion within Renton will be a Renton city park.

Chehalis–South Bay Trail
Though a railroad line is still active as of 1991, it may be abandoned in the near future. State Parks is interested in converting the right-of-way to a trail between Chehalis and South Bay.

Chelatchie Prairie Trail
Clark County in southeast Washington owns the right-of-way for a railroad line that runs from Vancouver east to Chelatchie near Yacolt. The line is used for an excursion train, and there are plans to put a trail alongside it as part of the Chinook Trail Project planned for the Columbia River Gorge.

Clayton Beach Trail
The proposed trail is located in Larrabee State Park and would be an extension of the Whatcom County Interurban Trail going south down to the beach.

Darrington Trail
Snohomish County Parks has plans to acquire the railroad right-of-way between Arlington and Darrington if the line is abandoned.

East Lake Sammamish Trail
The railroad along the east side of Lake Sammamish is still active, although it has only one shipper. King County Parks has plans to develop a trail along this route when it is abandoned.

Enumclaw Trail

The City of Enumclaw owns a railroad right-of-way through town and plans to make it into a trail.

Everett-Shoreline Interurban Trail

Snohomish County Parks has plans for developing a rail-trail along-side a proposed light-rail line between Everett and the King County border.

Iron Goat Trail

The Forest Service plans to develop a rail-trail along a right-of-way abandoned in 1910 on the west side of Stevens Pass. The trail should be open to the public in 1993.

Klickitat Trail

Klickitat County is interested in building a trail between Klickitat and Goldendale along a recently abandoned line.

Lacey–Offut Lake Trail

Thurston County has acquired the abandoned line between Lacey and Offut Lake for development of a multiple-use rail-trail.

Lake Union Bikeway

The City of Seattle plans to develop a trail along this right-of-way, which runs from the south end of Lake Union to Fishermen's Terminal.

North King County Interurban Trail

King County is planning development of a rail-trail on the old Interurban Railway right-of-way, which is owned and used by Puget Power and Light north to the Snohomish County line.

Palouse Pathway

Several groups are working to build a trail from Spokane to Pullman through the Palouse Hills along an abandoned line.

Sedro Wooley–Arlington Trail

Skagit County Parks is in the process of acquiring property to develop a rail-trail south from Sedro Wooley along an abandoned line to the Snohomish County line, just north of Arlington.

Similkameen Trail

The Department of Wildlife plans to build a trail along the Similkameen River in north-central Washington just west of Oroville.

Skagit River Trail

State Parks has acquired the abandoned line between Hamilton and Concrete for future trail development. The trail could be extended farther east to Rockport, where the old right-of-way comes out at Steelheaders Park.

Spokane–Newport Trail

In the Spokane area there is interest in a trail running north from Spokane to Newport along an abandoned railroad line.

White River–Palmer Trail

King County Parks plans to build a trail from the King County line at the White River north to Palmer. Part of this right-of-way has been abandoned, and the remaining part will be abandoned soon.

Woodard Bay Trail

The Department of Natural Resources has acquired the right-of-way between Woodard Bay and I-5 in Lacey and plans to develop it into a rail-trail.

Yelm–Tenino Trail

The railroad line between Yelm and Tenino will be abandoned in 1992, and Thurston County Parks plans to acquire it for a trail.

INDEX OF TRAILS BY SURFACE

Asphalt/concrete

Burke-Gilman Trail
Corridor Trail
Duwamish Bikeway
Issaquah Trail
King County Interurban Trail
Lower Yakima Pathway
Myrtle Edwards Park Trail
Neppel Landing Trail
Port Angeles
    Urban Waterfront Trail
Preston–Snoqualmie Trail
    (except one gravel
    switchback)
Seattle Waterfront Pathway
Snohomish–Arlington
    Centennial Trail
Spokane River Centennial Trail

Hard-packed gravel

Cowiche Canyon Trail
Issaquah Creek Trail
Lake Whatcom Trail
Laughing Jacob's Creek Trail
North Bend–Tanner Trail
Railroad Bikeway
South Bay Trail
Whatcom County Interurban
    Trail

Unimproved ballast

Ben Burr Trail
Douglas Creek Trail
Iron Horse State Park
Milwaukee Road Corridor Trail
Republic Rail-Trail
Scablands Nature Corridor
Snoqualmie Pass Trail
Snoqualmie Valley Trail

Dirt

Glacier–Maple Falls Trail
Lake Wilderness Trail
Old Robe Historic Trail
Pacific Crest Scenic Trail
Preston Railroad Trail
Spruce Railroad Trail
Sylvia Creek Trail
Wallace Falls Railway Grade
West Tiger Mountain
    Railroad Grade
Coal Creek Trail

INDEX

ABOUT
THE AUTHOR

Fred Wert spent much of his youth accompanying his father on steam engine rides all over the Northwest. An active bicyclist, hiker, and mountaineer, his outdoor activities and knowledge of railroads led him to explore rail-trails before many of them were actually developed. He was instrumental in the development of the Washington State Chapter of the Rails-to-Trails Conservancy and served as their first staff member. His work as a public facilities consultant includes rail-trail planning. He also serves on the board of the Washington Wildlife and Recreation Coalition and is the Planning Director for the Trans-Continental Trails Association. Fred has ridden all the rail-trails in the state, including a recently completed five-day ride between Plummer, Idaho, and Snoqualmie Pass.

ABOUT THE MOUNTAINEERS

The Mountaineers, founded in 1906, is a non-profit outdoor activity and conservation club, whose mission is *"to explore, study, preserve and enjoy the natural beauty of the outdoors...."* Based in Seattle, Washington, the club is now the third largest such organization in the United States, with 12,000 members and four branches throughout Washington State.

The Mountaineers sponsors both classes and year-round outdoor activities in the Pacific Northwest, which include hiking, mountain climbing, ski-touring, snowshoeing, bicycling, camping, kayaking and canoeing, nature study, sailing, and adventure travel. The club's conservation division supports environmental causes through educational activities, sponsoring legislation, and presenting informational programs. All club activities are led by skilled, experienced volunteers, who are dedicated to promoting safe and responsible enjoyment and preservation of the outdoors.

The Mountaineers Books, an active, non-profit publishing program of the club, produces guidebooks, instructional texts, historical works, natural history guides, and works on environmental conservation. All books produced by The Mountaineers are aimed at fulfilling the club's mission.

If you would like to participate in these organized outdoor activities or the club's programs, consider a membership in The Mountaineers. For information and an application, write or call: *The Mountaineers, Club Headquarters, 300 Third Avenue West, Seattle, Washington 98119; (206) 284-6310.*

OTHER BOOKS FROM THE MOUNTAINEERS

Send for catalog of more than 200 outdoor books published by:
The Mountaineers Books, 1011 SW Klickitat Way, Suite 107, Seattle, WA 98134.
1-(800) 553-4453